FV_

THE LAST OF THE MOHICANS

Civil Savagery and Savage Civility

TWAYNE'S MASTERWORK STUDIES

Robert Lecker, General Editor

THE LAST OF THE MOHICANS

Civil Savagery and Savage Civility

John McWilliams

TWAYNE PUBLISHERS • NEW YORK
Maxwell Macmillan Canada • *Toronto*
Maxwell Macmillan International • *New York Oxford Singapore Sydney*

Twayne's Masterwork Series No. 143

The Last of the Mohicans: Civil Savagery and Savage Civility
John McWilliams

Twayne Publishers
Macmillan Publishing Company
866 Third Avenue
New York, New York 10022

Maxwell Macmillan Canada, Inc.
1200 Eglinton Avenue East
Suite 200
Don Mills, Ontario M3C 3N1

Library of Congress Cataloging-in-Publication Data
McWilliams, John P.
    The last of the Mohicans : civil savagery and savage civility
John McWilliams.
        p.   cm. — (Twayne's masterwork studies : no. 143)
    Includes bibliographical references and index.
    ISBN 0-8057-8389-X. — ISBN 0-8057-4457-6 (pbk.)
    1. Cooper, James Fenimore, 1789–1851. Last of the Mohicans. 2. Historical fiction,
American—History and criticism. 3. Mohegan Indians in literature. 4. Noble savage in
literature. 5. United States—History—French and Indian War, 1755–1763—Literature
and the war. 6. Frontier and pioneer life—United States—Public opinion—History—
19th century. I. Title. II. Series.
PS1408.M37 1994
813'.2—dc20
                                                                                    94-14564
                                                                                    CIP

The paper used in this publication meets the minimum requirements of American
National Standard for Information Sciences—Permanence of Paper for Printed Library
Materials. ANSI Z3948-1984. ∞

10 9 8 7 6 5 4 3 2 1 (hc)
10 9 8 7 6 5 4 3 2 1 (pb)

Printed in the United States of America

For George Dekker

Contents

Illustrations

James Fenimore Cooper by John Wesley Jarvis (1780–1840), oil on canvas,
1822, 30" x 25"

New York State Historical Association, Cooperstown

Note on the References and Acknowledgments

Quotations from *The Last of The Mohicans* are from the revised World's Classics edition published by Oxford University Press in 1994 and edited by John McWilliams. This edition reprints the text established by James Sappenfield and E. N. Feltskog for *The Writings of James Fenimore Cooper*, published by the State University of New York Press. The edition also includes the three prefaces Cooper wrote for the 1826, 1831, and 1850 editions of the novel, as well as the 1850 preface to the Leatherstocking Tales. Parenthetical page references for quotations from these three prefaces also refer to the revised Oxford edition. Except as noted, all parenthetical quotations from assessments of Cooper's fiction in chapter 3, "The Critical Reception," are from *Fenimore Cooper: The Critical Heritage*, edited by G. Dekker and J. McWilliams (London: Routledge & Kegan Paul, 1973). Oxford University Press and Routledge & Kegan Paul have granted permission to quote from these two texts.

The New York State Historical Museum in Cooperstown has granted permission to reproduce Thomas Cole's painting *The Last of the Mohicans* (1827) and John Wesley Jarvis's portrait of Cooper (1822). The Hartford Atheneum has granted permission to reproduce John Vanderlyn's painting, *Death of Jane McCrea* (1804), which appears in chapter 5, "Race and Gender." Doubleday and Company has permitted duplication of the historical maps of Fort William Henry and of the Lake Champlain–Lake George corridor, to be found in chapter 6, "History and Empire." I have preserved two differences in the spelling of proper names: Cooper spelled Glens Falls as "Glenn's Falls" and Lieutenant Colonel George Monro's last name as "Munro."

For encouraging advice and for particular pieces of historical information, I would like to thank the participants in the 1993 Cooper Conference, especially Allan Axelrad, Hugh MacDougall, Geoffrey Rans, Alan Taylor, and James Wallace. Because a short, assimilative book canot develop its ideas by citing and arguing scholarship, I wish to acknowledge here my considerable debt to all works listed in the bibliography. The following reflections on a novel I continue to admire have all begun with ideas of insightful readers who have gone before.

J.M.

Chronology: James Fenimore Cooper's Life and Works

1757   At the southern tip of Lake George during the French and Indian War (1756–1763), British Lieutenant Colonel George Monro surrenders Fort William Henry and 2,500 British troops to the Marquis de Montcalm, a French general commanding a besieging force of 8,000 French regulars and 2,000 Indians.

1776–1783   The American Revolution.

1786   William Cooper, the novelist's father, establishes Cooperstown on lands at the southern tip of Lake Otsego. Cooper's lands, originally inhabited by the Iroquois, had been held by land speculator George Croghan under British title until the conclusion of the Revolutionary War.

1789   James Cooper born in Burlington, New Jersey. William Cooper moves his family to Cooperstown the following year. James grows up in Cooperstown; attends school in Albany.

1803   Cooper matriculates at Yale College; asked to leave two years later because of misconduct.

1806–1808   Sails before the mast to England and the Continent aboard the *Stirling*; serves as a midshipman in the U.S. Navy at Fort Oswego on Lake Ontario.

1811	Marries Susan Augusta De Lancey, daughter of a family of formerly prominent New York City Loyalists.
1811–1819	Lives as a gentleman farmer on family lands in Westchester County and in Cooperstown. Gradual depletion of Cooper family resources after the death of William Cooper in 1809.
1812–1815	War of 1812 against the British.
1820	Writes his first novel, *Precaution*, and, in the following year, *The Spy* (1821). *The Spy* becomes an international success.
1822–1826	Cooper moves to New York City and writes *The Pioneers* (1823), *The Pilot* (1824), *Lionel Lincoln* (1825), and *The Last of the Mohicans* (1826). His novels are published in both England and America, with translations into French, German, and other languages usually following promptly.
1824	President James Monroe, following a policy of Thomas Jefferson, supports the removal of eastern Indians to west of the Mississippi. Indian removal becomes controversial during the presidency of John Quincy Adams (1824–28). Forced Indian removal carried out with deathly effect by Presidents Jackson and Van Buren during the 1830s.
1826–1833	Appointed consul to Lyons, Cooper resides in Europe with his family. Lives most frequently in Paris but takes lengthy trips to England, the Low Countries, Switzerland, Germany, and Italy. Meets Walter Scott. Concern with and involvement in the European revolutionary movements of 1830. Writes *The Prairie* (1827), *The Red Rover* (1827), *Notions of the Americans* (1828), *The Wept of Wish-ton-Wish* (1829), and *The Water Witch* (1830). After 1830, turns to novels that concern European politics: *The Bravo* (1831), *The Heidenmauer* (1832), and *The Headsman* (1833).
1833–1836	Returns to America and resides in New York City. Political correspondent for the *Evening Post*. Writes *A Letter to His Countrymen* (1834) and *The Monikins* (1835). In Whig news-

papers Cooper begins to be attacked as an unpatriotic "aristo-crat" who wishes to put on foreign airs.

1836 — Returns to Cooperstown and remodels Otsego Hall, William Cooper's home.

1837–1838 — Publishes five volumes of sketches concerned with his European travels. Much-publicized controversy over the ownership and use of Three Mile Point on Lake Otsego. Writes *Homeward Bound* and *Home as Found* (1838). Lengthy libel suits against Whig editors begin. Writes a succinct summary of his political beliefs titled *The American Democrat* (1838) and the authoritative *History of the Navy of the United States* (1839).

1840 — Resumes writing novels about the frontier and the sea: *Mercedes of Castille* (1840), *The Two Admirals* (1842), *The Wing and Wing* (1842), *Wyandotté* (1843). Writes the last two Leatherstocking Tales, *The Pathfinder* (1840) and *The Deerslayer* (1841), which help restore his waning popularity.

1844–1846 — Tenants on large Hudson Valley estates forcibly revolt against paying rent. Cooper defends the landowner's position in the so-called Anti-Rent Wars by writing a trilogy titled The Littlepage Manuscripts: *Satanstoe* (1845), *The Chainbearer* (1846), and *The Redskins* (1846). Also writes *Afloat and Ashore* and *Miles Wallingford* (1844).

1847–1849 — Writes the first American utopian novel, *The Crater* (1847). Last frontier and sea novels: *Jack Tier* (1848), *The Oak Openings* (1848), and *The Sea Lions* (1849).

1850 — Prepares the Putnam Author's Revised Edition of his writings. Writes the preface to the Leatherstocking Tales and a novel about criminal law, *The Ways of the Hour*. Supports the Compromise of 1850, which enables the Union to survive at the expense of the North's accepting the Fugitive Slave Bill.

1851 — Dies in Cooperstown, leaving *The Towns of Manhattan* (also titled *New York*) unfinished.

1852   Memorial gathering for Cooper held in New York City, Daniel Webster presiding. Letters and tributes by Bancroft, Bryant, Emerson, Hawthorne, Irving, Longfellow, Melville, Parkman, Prescott, and Simms. The most impressive public celebration of an American writer's achievement yet held.

LITERARY AND
HISTORICAL CONTEXTS

1

Backgrounds and Foregrounds

The citizens of the nation in which James Fenimore Cooper was born, grew to maturity, and published his early novels (the United States of America from 1789 to 1830) were a self-conscious people who worriedly prided themselves on being an infant republic rather than a settled democracy. Few Americans would have denied that their New World was preparing to lead humanity in enacting God's laws of historical progress. America's emerging prominence was thought to rest on the twin blessings of having unlimited natural resources to the west and a limited government whose purpose was to guarantee individual freedoms. These two conditions—plenitude of nature and paucity of government—would permit a man to advance economically and ethically in accord with his abilities. The lasting external image of the nation, whether of 13 or 20 states, was of an expanding and prosperous agrarian economy dotted with towns, churches, and schools—one immense family farmland in which turnpikes and canals, steamboats and locomotives, mills and factories, would all serve as "internal improvements." The inner engine driving the nation's development was to be the secular spirit of Protestant Christianity, encouraging

Franklinian habits of Temperance, Industry, Order, and Thrift within the bounds of regard for one's community.

This vision of the national future, often offered as universally inclusive, was in fact tellingly exclusive. The claim that America was to serve as the world's melting pot dates from the 1780s, but descriptions of how assimilation would occur show that only immigrants of northern European stock were expected to be melted into the one national character. Nothing was then held in higher regard, both as an economic and as a moral value, than the nuclear family, but woman's sphere was both separate from and subordinate to man's. No matter how much a wife and mother may have toiled and nurtured, the advance of the family was publicly measured by male ownership of all domestic resources obtained through energies he had expended on the land or in the marketplace. In the 1830s, suspicion against all Catholics turned to violence, much as suspicion against French revolutionary "atheists" had done in the 1790s. The Jeffersonian ideal of America as a land of small independent farmers ironically proved to be far more applicable to northern and mid-Atlantic states than to the South, where large plantations and chattel slavery expanded rapidly after 1815. While blacks lived as a separate race within the bounds of the expanding nation, almost all Native Americans still lived, both by necessity and by choice, entirely outside of the United States. There were, of course, voices raised against these kinds of exclusions well before an era of reform movements began in the late 1830s. In general, however, the force of consensus meant that the phrase "the American," as we find it used during Cooper's lifetime, unconsciously connoted "white male Protestant."

There was, however, no consensus about desired leadership among the nation's varied white male Protestant groups. Just as most Americans presupposed that a Christian nation would emerge from establishing freedom of religion, so they assumed that equal rights would bring a natural aristocracy, rather than a social aristocracy, into positions of authority. Leaders would be chosen for their merit and talent, not because of political privilege accorded to any class or group. This truly revolutionary idea aroused rancor, however, as soon as it was applied to the institutions shaping daily life. During the early national period (1783–1815), the seaboard merchants, planters, educators and lawyers who formed the Federalist party believed in a strong patrician Senate, an appointive judiciary, suffrage restrictions, a strong navy, and even, in some instances, an established state church. The farmers, tradesmen, planters, educators, and lawyers who formed the Republican (later the Whig) party believed, by contrast, in a strong House of Representatives, an elective judiciary, turnpikes to the west, and moderate expansion of the suffrage. Neither party, however, was prepared to embrace the faith in the common man (the ordinary wage earner and small tradesman) that would characterize the politics of the era of Andrew Jackson, himself a good-size plantation owner. While Cooper was growing to maturity, the older notion of rule by an elected and educated elite chosen from leading families was still prevalent in both parties, as it was in the society as a whole. Citizens of the Republic treasured the right to elect people to govern them, but few Americans before the 1830s approved the democratic idea that the truth is to be found in the opinion of the majority.

In his fiction as well as his nonfiction, Cooper was to confront these issues with intensity and intelligence in part because his early years had been shaped by such tensions. James's father, William Cooper, a wheelwright born within no elite, had risen to great wealth and a seat in Congress by seizing the main financial chance amid the uncertainties of the western real estate market at the end of the Revolutionary War. James grew up among the beautiful hills, woods, and streams surrounding the growing frontier village of Cooperstown on Lake Otsego in central New York, but he also knew that the lands he roamed had originally been inhabited by the Oneida Iroquois and had then been sold to the British, before they passed into the hands of William Cooper for purposes of both sale to incoming settlers and preservation of a family estate. The young man who delighted in the forest was also a gentleman's son raised to learn his Latin, to associate with the sons of Federalist families, to attend Yale College, and to "marry well"—in sum, to assume the privileged position of responsibility to which he was born. But when James Cooper began to write novels at the age of 31, he did so not in order to outdo an unnamed British woman novelist (as family myth long maintained) but because the family fortune in land and in cash was suddenly and forever gone. Writing became for him more than a gentleman's way of apprehending truth through words. Like the Indians with whose fate he sympathized, James had been dispossessed of his birthright in land. To write salable fiction could serve as an alternative mode of entrepreneurship, of reaffirming what it might still mean to become "James Fenimore Cooper" through one's own literary industry and resolve.

From such origins came the productive inner and outer conflicts that would sustain 32 novels and many volumes of social commentary. Allthough Cooper would defend the white European idea that a paper deed could certify land ownership, he would also show that the violent dispossession of the Indian was an injustice exposing civilization's pretension to virtue. While struggling to express the Beauty and the Terror of the unspoiled wilderness ("the Sublime," as it was then called), he would also praise the pastoral prosperity of farming communities, and even at times sound hospitable to a future of industrial progress. Proud of his republican beliefs, Cooper would praise equality of legal right as the essence of the New World's superiority. Yet Cooper would also create or reaffirm racial stereotypes in his fictional characters and worry publicly that the election of men from lower classes was ipso facto a sign of the demagoguery that would bring down the educated gentry.

The easy, mindless response to such anomalies is simply to condescend to Cooper as an inconsistent thinker or, worse yet, to dismiss him as a privileged and racist dead white male. The fact is that these very inconsistencies, updated in reference, remain as much ours as they were his. We wish to have pristine wilderness and gleaming cities, family farms and cheap supermarkets, ethnic pluralism and racial integration, industrial prosperity and a pure environment, presidents who will be "of the people" yet somehow beyond them. White Americans wish to drive for a brief visit to an Indian reservation in the safe comfort of a Pontiac, a Winnebago RV, or a Cherokee jeep. Like Cooper, we wish to believe that we treat all people equally, yet our first way of sizing up another individual is often to classify that person by race, gender, and class. The origins of the nation, as reflected in Cooper's writings, are based on conflicts of value we have clearly not resolved. If the present or next generation will have to make the hard choices, will we or they be any more prepared to make them than Cooper was?

The literary context Cooper faced in 1820 was as perplexingly open as the nation's political or economic future. America's British heritage posed vexing contrarities. Although Americans had recently fought the British twice in order to establish their independence, they simultaneously felt that Shakespeare and Milton, Pope and Wordsworth, belonged as much to them as to any Londoner. English was the Americans' mother tongue, but England itself was the old monarchical skin that young America had supposedly outgrown and violently cast aside. A colonial literary culture needed to be superseded through still unknown literary means. Americans were searching to create works of literary maturity that would justify their rebellion against the British father and prove their cultural maturity as the New World's sovereign republic. Yet the credible sign of American literary success would be critical recognition—and profitable sales—back in England as well as at home.

Seeking British approval for American literary works that claimed to supersede British culture created a double standard that would remain in force until the Civil War, and not fully disappear until World War I. But the problem was especially acute during the decade following 1815. Despite the British burning of Washington D.C., Americans celebrated the inconclusive War of 1812 as a nativist victory as soon as Jackson defeated the British at the Battle of New Orleans. A burst of expansive nationalism grew out of the sudden awareness that the British presence in all lands west of the 19 United States was now gone forever. While the nation's literary prospects seemed limitless, the nation's literary achievement was still vexingly delayed. Forty years had passed since America's declaration of independence, much literature had been written, and precious little had been achieved. No American author had yet sustained a literary career in dollars and through time. There was no adequate copyright law protecting a beginning American writer against cheaply reprinted editions of British works. American literary periodicals, like the notoriety of poets, dramatists, and writers of fiction, had repeatedly foundered after an initial success. If as F. Scott Fitzgerald claims there are no second acts in American literature, in 1820 it seemed that the world's audience had been waiting overtime for the first act to begin.

Contrary to long-standing belief, there had been a great deal of American fiction before Cooper, including adaptations of *Don Quixote* by Hugh Henry Brackenridge and Tabitha Tenney, widely read novels of seduction and betrayal by Hannah Foster and Suzannah Rowson, and the Gothic romances of Charles Brockden Brown. Even though Cooper would write a fleeting tribute to Brockden Brown, he at first turned his back on native literature by writing a purportedly British novel of manners (titled *Precaution*) somewhat in the manner of Jane Austen. His next novel, *The Spy* (1822) established his reputation on both sides of the Atlantic. In the setting, characters, and doubled protagonists of *The Spy*, Cooper found the kind of fiction which he would pursue for the remainder of his career. His best novels, including *The Last of the Mohicans*, would be adaptations of the kind of historical novel first made world-famous by Walter Scott's *Waverley* (1815) and its sequels. In Cooper's hands, as we shall see, the historical novel became in part an adventure romance, emphasizing men's physical confrontations with sea and forest frontiers. And yet by evoking particular places and events in the regional and national past, Cooper's fictions would always remain a way for his newly independent people to summon up those historical associations by which their identity could be defined.

Cooper's initial indebtedness to Scott's form of fiction, combined with his distrust of Scott's aristocratic politics, would lead Cooper to resent the label "the American Scott" that was promptly fastened upon him. Nonetheless, despite all the changes Cooper made in Scott's form, there is a deeper sense in which the label is both fair and commendatory. Like Scott, Cooper wrote as an educated gentleman looking back across the upheavals of the French and American revolutions at times of national and cultural origin. Both authors sought to assess their country's present by a cumulative and comprehensive fictional study of its past. Both were defensively proud of their allegiance to a regional culture (Scotland and America) still clearly dependent on England. Unlike Scott, however, Cooper knew he needed to prove the worth of his writing on both sides of the ocean. In the literary climate of the 1820s,

American literature could ironically be well received only by adapting British forms to American subjects. Cooper was not alone among his contemporaries in confronting this irony. The beginnings of a rich tradition of American nature poetry can be traced to the *Poems* (1817) of William Cullen Bryant, who was called "the American Wordsworth." The seemingly easy whimsy in the short stories and familiar essays of Washington Irving's *The Sketch Book* (1820) would continue in the work of American authors as diverse as Nathaniel Hawthorne and E. B. White, Henry James and Lewis Thomas. In his own era, however, Irving was regarded as "the American Spectator," "the American Addison," or, slightly later, "the American Lamb." Throughout the opening decades of the nineteenth century, when "imitation" of an admired earlier writer was still common practice, such comparisons surely seemed less condescending to American authors than they do now. Pouring new wine into old skins, we need to remind ourselves, can be the best and only way to market it.

2

The Importance of
The Last of the Mohicans

Assessing the "importance" of any written text remains a slippery business. What standards does one apply? Is importance to be measured by long-standing popularity or intrinsic literary merit? Whenever sales figures and evidence about reprintings are available, numbers can be offered to show how extensively a text has been available and has sold, though not how widely it has been read. We can presume, though not prove, that continued large sales, together with lasting inclusion in the academic literary canon, show that a book has been absorbed as a part of its people's culture, that it has shaped readers' attitudes if not their conduct. But is a text's cultural prominence all we mean when we speak of its importance? Do we not also imply that this particular book is somehow more insightful, better written, more powerful in its effect on us, than thousands of other books gathering library dust? This second measure of a text's importance rests on our appreciation of its literary art, the originality of its ideas, the depth and complexity of the imagined world it creates for us. In this sense, the book's importance rests on special intrinsic qualities that enable us to feel that this book is somehow truly superior, worth preserving, even perhaps a "master-work," as Twayne's series title confidently proclaims.

Determining this second kind of importance need not, however, be a wholly subjective act. In reviews, letters, and recorded conversation, later writers have attested to the reasons why a particular text has been important to them. Individual talents thus derive their importance from their place in a literary tradition. Similarly, schools of criticism insist on their own particular standards by which quality of writing should be judged. These kinds of assessments are never dismissible, but neither are they definitive. Gloom-sayers who now prophesy the death of literature argue that no book will be important once print culture has finally succumbed to audiovisual media. But anyone who wants to understand how the past has made the present will always have to discriminate among the millions of books produced by a five-century avalanche of the printed word. That is why the importance of a work of literature remains a vital question, even though, like all else in life, responding to it involves a muddled combining of external fact and subjective judgment.

By all external measures, *The Last of the Mohicans* has retained the authority of constant presence. Never out of print since its publication, it has been translated into Japanese, Chinese, Arabic, and every major European language. There are 17 English editions of the novel currently in print. The fourth widely viewed film version of *The Last of the Mohicans*, starring Daniel Day-Lewis as Hawkeye and Russell Means as Chingachgook, was released in 1992. Frank Luther Mott, who completed the first informed study of American book sales, listed *The Last of the Mohicans* among the 21 best-selling American books through 1947. Hawkeye was the name given to the hero of "M*A*S*H," perhaps the most popular of all American television series, including "Cheers." The book's highly visual qualities have attracted painters and illustrators from Thomas Cole through N. C. Wyeth to Classic Comics. Cooper's book has been read and admired by authors as dissimilar as George Sand and D. H. Lawrence, Francis Parkman and Maxim Gorky, Honoré de Balzac and Willa Cather. *The Last of the Mohicans* is one of those books everyone knows something about, even when one has not read it. Despite its faults, it remains inescapably here.

Literary works of intrinsic importance accommodate and reward the shifting interests of successive generations. To its earliest readers, *The Last of the Mohicans* was the first novel to prove that excellent historical fiction could be fashioned from a fledgling frontier nation supposed to lack all history. As Cooper's five-novel sequence unfolded, *The Last of the Mohicans* was rightly seen as the novel in which Leatherstocking, so often considered the embodiment of the American hero, first became dominant and grandly admirable. Later readers found it a compelling adventure story that could serve as a prototype for westerns of all kinds from the dime novels of the 1870s to "The Lone Ranger" of the 1950s. Set a loner hero and his red sidekick out into the unknown, rescuing maidens and righting wrongs, silhouetted against a panorama of nature's sublimity, and you have a two-century recipe for popular success, be it in drugstore fiction, TV serials, or G-rated feature-length violence. Cooper's novel has also, however, been a source of stillness antithetical to melodrama. Lovers of wilderness and of painting have found in Cooper's verbal landscapes a perfect medium, readily transferable to canvas, for conveying the immensity of unspoiled nature.

Above all, however, *The Last of the Mohicans* has been important for its portrayal of the clash between red and white cultures. The world's image of the "Red Man" undoubtedly owes more to Cooper's novel than to any other single written text. For good and for bad, Uncas and Magua, opposed faces of one figure, have dominated white thinking about the character of the Indian from Cooper's time to ours. To earlier generations, Cooper's portrayal of the Indian was important primarily because of the extent to which the Leatherstocking novels did or did not justify the demise—some said the inevitable extinction—of the red race. Since the resurgence of Native American cultures during the "Red Power" movement of the 1970s, the melancholy contemplation of "the last of" various Native American peoples has lost much, though by no means all, of its emotional resonance (witness the recent fascination for the demise of the Guanahani during the 1992 Columbus commemorations). We may even say that the power of Cooper's novel, has not appreciably lessened, in part because current literary and scholarly interest in issues of race, gender, and cultural origin is well suited to Cooper's way of characterizing people. His fictions engage us in exactly the kind of "identity politics" currently in academic and cultural fashion: a person's race, gender, class and ethnic origin are thought to account for his or her traits and opinions.[1] Individuals represent racial and generic groups. As these representative characters clash in the pre-Revolutionary wilderness, Cooper's reader experiences a version of the founding of a new culture that was to become "America." However much we may protest against the stereotypical or even "racist" conclusions Cooper may draw, his racially and socially determined way of thinking about the establishment of cultural power seems remarkably contemporary.

When Cooper was preparing final revisions of *The Last of the Mohicans*, he regarded the book, no longer as a separate novel, but as the second of the Leatherstocking Tales, now reordered in the chronological sequence of their hero's life. What binds the five novels together is not only the presence of Leatherstocking but also the bond formed between the white hero and the red, Natty Bumppo and Chingachgook, a bond that shapes the plot in all the tales except *The Prairie*. Their friendship, discussed compellingly by D. H. Lawrence, raises questions as troublingly important in the 1990s as in the 1820s. Why is it that the deepest relationship in the capacious world of the Leatherstocking Tales is an interracial, wholly asexual, and often wordless bond between two males? What status can such a friendship have within either white or red culture? Does the intensity of an interracial friendship depend on its alienation from both races? What does such a male bond imply about the way "civilized" society privileges a marriage between man and woman, whether they be of one race or of two? And finally, what is the worth of red and white cultures if their most admirable representatives can exist only apart from both of them? In the superb closing chapter of *The Last of the Mohicans*, as Chingachgook and Hawkeye—both weeping—clasp hands over the grave of Uncas, all of these questions become powerfully real in ways that will resonate for the reader through the entire five-novel series.

3

The Critical Reception

The pre-Romantic belief that fiction was an artistically inferior and/or morally corrupting kind of literature lingered on in the America of the 1820s. During the European Renaissance, critical theorists had regarded epic poetry as the highest of literary genres, and prose fiction as the lowest. The Puritan heritage had led New Englanders to suspect that imagining a world was the Devil's work. Four of America's Founding Fathers and prominent Enlightenment thinkers—Washington, Franklin, Jefferson, and John Adams—all felt that fiction was so unscientific, so contrary to Reason, that it should be read sparingly by everyone and not at all by the many young women then avidly reading novels of seduction. Instead of challenging these prejudices against fiction, Cooper worked around them. He introduced his first novels as mere "tales," with no professed design upon the reader beyond entertainment. The genteel love stories Cooper unfolds in unlikely frontier settings are in part his attempt to reclaim and redirect the interests of an existing readership among women. Only after acquiring an international reputation was he to write prefaces and public letters acknowledging his ambitious concerns both as a historical romancer and as a writer of social criticism in fiction.

The Critical Reception

In his second preface to *The Last of the Mohicans*, written for a British edition of 1831, Cooper advanced large claims for his novel's portrayal of racial conflict:

> The Mohicans were the possessors of the country first occupied by the Europeans in this portion of the continent. They were, consequently, the first dispossessed; and the seemingly inevitable fate of all these people, who disappear before the advances, or it might be termed the inroads of civilisation, as the verdure of their native forests falls before the nipping frost, is represented as having already befallen them. There is sufficient historical truth in the picture to justify the use that has been made of it. (9)

Although escape and pursuit sequences may occupy the foreground of the reader's attention, *The Last of the Mohicans* is intended to be a novel about the "dispossessed." As we read, the Mohican tribe will often seem to represent all Indian peoples and the process of their dispossession will convey a general "historical truth." Cooper is well aware that white Americans have long justified the dispossession of the Indian on the grounds that white "civilization," with its books, churches, houses, and farms, is superior to red "savagery." His language acknowledges the prevalence of the white view but immediately suggests an alternative. If the "advances" of civilization might better be termed "inroads," is it not utterly false to assume that the "progress" of civilization demands the extinction of the savage? Perhaps the white man's westward advance is not so much a divinely decreed conquest as an invasion. At the outset Cooper identifies the Indians as "the possessors" of the country, not merely its inhabitants. "Their native forests" are replaced by a civilization unexpectedly likened to a "nipping frost" that brings wintry blight. The pattern of this passage—offering a subversive alternative within apparent approval of white values—recurs again and again in the novel's plot, characterization, and language.

The first reviewers of any book, who must respond to the timing of publishing markets, are likely to react only to its more apparent surfaces. *The Last of the Mohicans* was greeted, not surprisingly, with widespread approval in American and European journals. Not only was Cooper already a world-famous author. His novel satisfied a recent critical demand, expressed often in prominent journals like the *North American Review*, for an American Walter Scott who would write historical romances on the "era of the Indian wars" showing Red Men to be simultaneously both "a highly poetical people" and "savage warriors."[2] The early celebrity of *The Last of the Mohicans* was based primarily, however, on a response that we, in our fast-paced world of instant gratification, can no longer share. Although twentieth-century readers complain that Cooper's plot develops in too leisurely a manner, Cooper's contemporaries were astonished by its "intense and breathless interest; there is no break, no pause, no abiding place of rest; but we are urged incessantly forward by an irresistible power, hurrying on to the final catastrophe" (109). Another reviewer even spoke of Cooper's narrative as "the visions of a long and feverish dream" in which our "excitement cannot be controlled" because "we are borne through strange and fearful, and even agonizing scenes of doubt, surprise, danger and sudden deliverance" (90). The "excitement" such readers felt clearly depended on two things: repeated sequences of escape, pursuit, and recapture and the fear of Indian vengeance (sudden assault, scalping, arson, threatened rape) against white characters whose insecurities the reader is invited to share. For the casual nineteenth-century reader, Cooper plainly knew how to turn racial fear into a gripping read. For the twentieth-century reader, Cooper's willingness to use fear of savagery as the driving force of the plot conflicts with his readiness to expose the injustice of the white man's "inroads."

A major issue for early reviewers was the degree of "Verisimilitude" (the word *Realism* was then unknown) in a novel that clearly made use of the atmospheric coloring and marvelous incidents of the romance, both Gothic and historical. Some of the worry now seems trivial. Was it not absurd, reviewers claimed, that Cora and Alice Munro would even try to visit their father's fort in the midst of a war-torn wilderness? (In fact, there was historical precedent for it.) What motive could the tiresome New England psalmodist David Gamut possibly have for joining a British war party in New York? Don't the tracking feats of Leatherstocking, Uncas, and Chingachgook strain our credibility (a fact Mark Twain would later turn into hilarious satire)? Could a strong commander like Colonel Munro be so instantly transformed into a shattered imbecile by just one atrocity, even if it is a massacre following the surrender of his fort? Such concern about incidentals is in fact an odd form of tribute; it shows us how well, in the main, Cooper had succeeded in suspending his reader's disbelief.

The deeper issue of accuracy centered on Cooper's portrayal of the Indian. The terms of the controversy are themselves revealing. Cooper was not faulted—as we would surely fault him today—for not knowing enough factual detail about the religion, language, economy, and daily life of the Iroquois and the Delaware. Instead, he was criticized for being overly sympathetic toward the Indian and for idealizing the Indian character. Again and again, critics protest that Uncas is an impossibly handsome, overly chivalric, and unconvincingly "noble" savage, while remaining silent about any possible excess in Cooper's portrayal of the deviltry of Magua. Even Francis Parkman, great historian though he was, protested as late as 1852 that "the young Mohican, Uncas, . . . does not at all resemble a genuine Indian. Magua, the villain of the story, is a less untruthful portrait" (255).

The ironies latent in this long-standing charge are remarkable. In 1820 the only detailed recent account of eastern Indian life known to white audiences had been written by John Heckewelder, a Moravian missionary who had great respect for the Delaware. Reviewing *The Spy* for the *North American Review*, W. H. Gardiner had urged Cooper to authenticate a novel concerning the Indian wars by using "the flattering pictures of their best historian, the indefatigable Heckewelder" (62). After Cooper had written *The Last of the Mohicans*, using Heckewelder as his main source for Indian customs, Gardiner then ridiculed Cooper for having "relied exclusively upon the narrations of the enthusiastic and visionary Heckewelder" (112). One year later, Lewis Cass, a future Secretary of State and Presidential candidate, attacked the accuracy of Cooper's Indians relentlessly, concluding that Cooper had "consulted the book of Mr. Heckewelder, instead of the book of nature" (8). This often repeated charge so rankled Cooper that, when he wrote the preface to the Leatherstocking

Tales more than 20 years later, he felt a need to challenge and refute it by arguing that, whereas Heckewelder had actually lived among the Indians, the only Red Men most of his critics knew anything about were the degraded Indians seen among whites at land sales and treaty conferences. As Cooper surely suspected, there had always been more than racial prejudice behind the attack on his "idealized" Indians. At a time when Indians were being forcibly removed from lands east of the Mississippi, it was uncomfortable—-to say the least—to have a writer of Cooper's stature conveying too "flattering" an image of the savage.

By midcentury Cooper had become widely regarded, in a phrase used by both Washington Irving and Herman Melville, as "our national novelist" (37, 244). Among the many summary tributes written soon after Cooper's death, the essays by Francis Parkman and George Sand are especially important, both because of their intrinsic merit and because the difference between them raises an issue central to *The Last of the Mohicans*. Parkman and Sand recognized that, more than any previous author, Cooper had impressed the lonely experience of wilderness, both as a sublime landscape painting and as a terror of the unknown, on the minds of European and American readers. In Parkman's phrase, Cooper had been unexcelled at conveying the "sombre poetry of solitude and danger" (256). But the conclusion they believe Cooper would have us draw from the confrontation of races differs greatly. Parkman rightly concludes that novels like *The Last of the Mohicans*, dwelling on the "carnage fields" of European colonial warfare, confirm the great truth that "Civilization has a destroying as well as a creating power" (251–52). But as a patriotic American historian and Harvard-educated patrician, Parkman also claims that Cooper's Indian characters—especially Uncas—are "for the most part either superficially or falsely drawn" (252). Parkman fears the destructive power of Civilization because it spells the end of the wilderness, not because it might exterminate the red man. When Parkman recalls his visit to Glens Falls, where much of the novel's first volume takes place, he regrets that "mills, factories and bridges have marred the native wildness of the spot, and a village has usurped the domain of the forest" (257). The last of the Mohicans, whether Uncas or Chingachgook, is of no more lasting concern to Parkman, however, than he is to most present-day denizens of Lake George's Mohican Motel.

As a European and a feminist, George Sand felt no need to minimize the racial injustice that Cooper's novel had made her feel. She argues that "Cooper was able, without too great an affront to the pride of his country, to plead the cause of the Indians" and insists that, like Leatherstocking, "the Mohican is also a great imaginative figure." For her, Cooper's purpose in describing the "Homeric virtues, fearful nobility and sublime barbarity" of Indian life was to free his countrymen to admit that "in order to be what we are, we had to kill a great people and devastate a mighty land" (267). The Leatherstocking Tales ultimately signify more than the Waverley novels, Sand believes, because more is at stake in them: "He [Scott] mourns for a nation, a power, above all an aristocratic way of life. What Cooper sings for and laments is a noble people exterminated; a serene natural world laid waste; he mourns all nature and all mankind" (268). George Sand can tell us why it has always been so much more difficult for a white American than for a European fully to face the crime done to the Indian: "An American was bound to be reluctant to stigmatise those iniquities from which the very strength and independence of his people had been born" (266).

Just as children often define their separate identity by rebelling against parents, so many a writer turns upon the dominant figures of the preceding literary generation. So it was with the Leatherstocking Tales, which dropped out of sophisticated literary discourse in the late nineteenth century, perhaps because they were then at the height of their popularity among general readers. Mark Twain, self-proclaimed exposer of all pretense, sought to forever demolish Cooper's authority by ridiculing the errors of his adventure-romance. The Leatherstocking Tales were ably parodied by Thackeray and Bret Harte. They were then cheapened into the formulas of the western dime novel (solitary gun-toting hero with aid of Indian auxiliary kills all villains and departs into the sunset). *The Last of the Mohicans* was repeatedly abridged and its style "simplified" for younger readers, who were soon to prefer comic book and film versions anyway. Only Joseph Conrad, who admired Cooper's sea fiction and was certainly not afraid of romance, insisted that Cooper's "art is genuine" because "the road to legitimate realism is through poetical feeling" (288). Conrad's observation that "for James Fenimore Cooper nature was not the framework, it was an essential part of existence" (287) concisely captures the power that the forest of *The Last of the Mohicans* exerts on both characters and readers.

In establishing American literature as a worthy tradition separable from England, no book has been more important than D. H. Lawrence's lively *Studies in Classic American Literature* (1923). Especially concerned with issues of race, inner rebellion, and what he calls "the spirit of place," Lawrence devotes 2 of 12 chapters to Cooper.[3] Cooper's fictional Indians lead Lawrence unknowingly to reaffirm a prophecy made in council speeches by such prominent historical chiefs as Dragging Canoe, Tecumseh, and Seattle: "The demon of the place and the unappeased ghosts of the dead Indians act within the unconscious or under-conscious soul of the white American" (41). Both Magua and Uncas, Lawrence perceives, should be seen as imagined creations that derive from white guilt over racial dispossession. With less plausibility, Lawrence argues that Cooper is so fearful of interracial love and marriage that he simply kills off Uncas and Cora. In Lawrence's view, Cooper can finally value only two kinds of alienated and barren virtue. On the one hand, there is the Leatherstocking: "an isolate, almost selfless, stoic, enduring man, who lives by death, by killing, but who is pure white" (69). On the other hand, there is the bond formed at the end of *The Last of the Mohicans* between Leatherstocking and Chingachgook, "the stark, loveless, wordless unison of two men who have come to the bottom of themselves" (59). For Lawrence, Cooper's creativity derives from his suppressed alienation both from the Red Man's blood-knowledge and from the white man's materialistic "progress." Hawkeye and the Big Serpent ultimately return us, Lawrence darkly concludes, to the clean competence of the perfect kill: "The essential American soul is hard, isolate, stoic and a killer. It has never yet melted" (68).

Since Lawrence's time, more than 100 books on Cooper and over 40 articles on *The Last of the Mohicans* have been published. Scholar-critics who wish to define traditions of American fiction regularly include or begin with a chapter on Cooper; richly detailed books studying the five Leatherstocking Tales have recently been published. To summarize the scholarship on *The Last of the Mohicans* adequately would be impossible here. One can, however, identify central critical issues that are likely to affect our reading of the novel. Following Lawrence, many readers have regarded The Leatherstocking Tales as a long romance having less to do with American history or frontier settlement than with the dark lives that lie both within the self and beyond known geographic bounds. Others have contended that Cooper's fiction retains descriptive authority both as a sequence of "historical novels" and as a grand example of social criticism through fiction. Just as Scott's fictions can be read both as historical novels and as historical romances, so *The Last of the Mohicans* can be—and has been read as a persuasive record of pre-Revolutionary imperial warfare as well as an expression of Cooper's (or America's) cultural prejudices and inner psychological tensions. A third, much less common approach has been to regard *The Last of the Mohicans* as salable entertainment, a putting together of motifs from different literary genres in an especially compelling form. The world of The Leatherstocking Tales has continued to be a capacious one, recently attracting readings by critics of Deconstructionist, Marxist, Feminist, and New Historicist persuasions.

Despite the variety of critical approaches, readings of the novel continue to raise simple-sounding questions that are in fact vexingly difficult to answer. Is this novel, this "narrative of 1757," meant to be read as insight into history, or is it an incredible forest fantasy, "a long and feverish dream," written down by James Fenimore Cooper in his study? Are Cooper's characters stereotypical because they illustrate his own prejudices, or his society's prejudices, or because stereotypes themselves contain an important element of truth? What is the connection Cooper perceives between the white man's growing, guilty appreciation of untouched wilderness and the presumed end of red culture? As Lawrence angrily put it, "Can you make a land virgin by killing off its aborigines?" (40).

The one unchanging response to the Leatherstocking Tales has been admiration for Cooper's characterization of Leatherstocking himself. One of the few convincingly heroic characters in post-Enlightenment literature, Natty Bumppo has somehow won the affection of even those writers who, like Thackeray, Harte, and Twain, are especially bent on demolishing Cooper through parody. No monster of virtue, Leatherstocking has his prejudices and his failings (he is verbose and vain on more than one occasion), but his honest love of all things natural gives to his criticisms of society's hypocrisies a ring of authority. Much critical comment on Leatherstocking has affirmed Cooper's final summary of him as "a character that possessed little of civilization but its highest principles as they are exhibited in the uneducated, and all of savage life that is not incompatible with these great rules of conduct" (396). Balzac, for instance, claimed that Leatherstocking was "a magnificent moral hermaphrodite, born of the savage state and of civilization, who will live as long as literatures last" (196). Although twentieth-century readers are more likely to perceive the waste of heroic qualities in Cooper's often melancholy and alienated hero, who belongs to neither red nor white culture, the impact of Natty Bumppo's character seems not to have diminished. Walt Whitman may yet prove right to have exclaimed that Leatherstocking was "from everlasting to everlasting" (36). Readers of *The Last of the Mohicans*, however, should beware of softening Hawkeye into some kind of wilderness knight forever lost in wonder at nature's God. Unlike later novels in the series, *The Last of the Mohicans* unflinchingly confronts the reasons why pathfinding compels the finest of men to become, as Lawrence says, "hard, isolate, stoic and a killer" (68).

A READING

4

Style and Gender

Although the issues of race and power raised by *The Last of the Mohicans* remain fully contemporary, Cooper's prose style and the genres to which his novel belongs became forever separate from us during the ages of Realism and Modernism (1870–1940). Realists like Mark Twain, Kate Chopin, and Stephen Crane, and Modernists like Ernest Hemingway and Sherwood Anderson, demanded short, simple words, accuracy of description, and natural spoken dialogue. They regarded intricate plots based on suspense, adventure, horror or withheld information as at best distracting and at worst so silly as to seem incredible. Characters should resemble "real people" who speak ordinary language in everyday circumstances; nothing suspiciously sensational should ever happen to them. Concision, brevity, and unstated irony became the writer's desired goals. Instead of judging characters, novelists were asked to render them with such dramatic immediacy that the writer would seem to recede entirely from the imagined world he or she was creating. Elaborate descriptions with lots of adjectives were out. Throw away the fancy five dollar word (*engender*) and find the nickel word that does the same job better (*make*).

Although our Postmodernist era has in its turn challenged many of these goals as superficial and barren, we continue to bring Realist assumptions to the reading of fiction, perhaps because television thrives on simple words and immediate images. In reading a novelist like James Fenimore Cooper, therefore, we must at the outset confront differences of style. Cooper wrote elaborate descriptive prose for a generation accustomed to reading for long periods of time. His syntax varies from elaborate five-line sentences containing many dependent clauses to single-line sentences in which subject precedes verb precedes object, very much in the manner Mark Twain approved. Cooper's is the narrative voice of an informed and rational gentleman who, like his British and Scottish predecessors Henry Fielding and Walter Scott, comments on his fictive world with seeming control and good judgment, though not omniscience. Although Cooper's plot may be intricate, it often seems to serve primarily as a thread for sewing in gorgeous descriptive passages that are not at all ornamental, but central to the author's purpose. Cooper's narrator uses both a self-consciously Latinate and a bluntly Anglo-Saxon vocabulary. His diction assumes that he—and therefore his presumed reader—are well-educated whites whose ability to absorb a wide range of diction (from "the Apollonian aborigine" to "the Indian" to "the screechin' imp" or from "the luminary" to "God's candle" to "the sun") combines a great interest in the variety of language with an awareness of how dialect serves, rightly or wrongly, to separate people by social class.

Three passages from the novel's opening chapters—one of exposition, one of natural description, one of narrative—may serve to introduce both the difficulties and the merits of Cooper's prose. The first chapter of *The Last of the Mohicans* opens with the following paragraph:

> It was a feature peculiar to the colonial wars of North America, that the toils and dangers of the wilderness were to be encountered, before the adverse hosts could meet. A wide, and, apparently, an impervious boundary of forests, severed the possessions of the hostile provinces of France and England. The hardy colonist, and the trained European who fought at his side, fre-

quently expended months in struggling against the rapids of the streams, or in effecting the rugged passes of the mountains, in quest of an opportunity to exhibit their courage in more martial conflict. But, emulating the patience and self-denial of the practised native warriors, they learned to overcome every difficulty, and, it would seem, that in time, there was no recess of the woods so dark, nor any secret place so lovely, that it might claim exemption from the inroads of those who had pledged their blood to satiate their vengeance, or to uphold the cold and selfish policy of the distant monarchs of Europe. (15)

By specifying neither year nor place, the paragraph sums up the essence of American colonial warfare in general, of which the following 32 chapters of "narrative" will provide one historical example. Cooper's long paragraph consists of only four increasingly lengthy, but always orderly sentences made up of abstract words that present people as generic types ("the hardy colonist," "the trained European," etc.). The author's perspective is as wide, his tone as magisterial, as the importance of an entire continent allows. But his attitudes, when the passage is examined closely, do not uphold the patriotism and defense of civilization that the style leads one to expect. By emphasizing the trials of penetrating the wilderness, Cooper suggests that there is something insane in the sending of armies many miles and many months into the unknown so that they might fight one another to the death. An entire heroic code threatens to collapse into vanity when we are told that all these soldiers are seeking merely "an opportunity to exhibit their courage." At paragraph's end, we learn that behind any military glory such armies might achieve lies "the cold and selfish policy of the distant monarchs of Europe." The only lasting effect that colonial wars are said to have is that the "lovely" recesses of the woods are metaphorically and literally transgressed by "inroads."

Does Cooper seek to undermine French and British colonial imperialism because both European nations would, a short 20 years later, lose "their" lands to the more progressive republic of the United States of America? It initially seems so, especially because Cooper concludes his introductory remarks three paragraphs later by insisting that "the incidents we shall attempt to relate occured during the third year of the war which England and France last waged, for the possession of a country, that neither was destined to retain" (17). In fact, however, Cooper permits no national patriotism about the failure of European colonialism. His first paragraph rightly notes that "the hardy colonist" served as a provincial militiaman alongside the British regular. Thus, the colonial American was also seeking his own opportunity to display courage; he also has succeeded only in making an inroad upon lovely places. Just as the European regulars fought to uphold the selfish policies of European kings, so the colonists "pledged their blood to satiate their vengeance," presumably against French Catholics and their Indian allies. The colonists' conduct may have been "hardy" but their motive was no more admirable. And so, while emphasizing the futility of taking and losing, retaking and relosing, the same series of forts in the wilderness, Cooper gives us a summary experience of an ordinary soldier who is neither French, British, nor American, but any and all three of them simultaneously: "the echoes of the mountains threw back the laugh, or repeated the wanton cry, of many a gallant and reckless youth, as he hurried by them [the defeated bands of retreating soldiers] in the noontide of his spirits, to slumber in a long night of forgetfulness" (16–17).

Violation, violence, and death on all hands are the facts to which Cooper's opening paragraphs introduce us. The soldier's noontide of thoughtless cheer is followed abruptly and inexplicably by an eternal night of being forgotten. Nothingness and silence, silence and nothingness, await them all. The historian in Cooper thus sets a tone that the adventure-romancer in Cooper promptly challenges. After opening his novel with this sweeping perspective on the oblivion of history, Cooper will proceed to do all he can to make us care about the survival of a few individuals who are glimpsed, as if by a zoom lens narrowing into the forest, near Lake George during a few days of August 1757.

The second passage, one of Cooper's most justly famous, is of an utterly different kind. During the 1820s, the group of painters later known as the Hudson River School—Thomas Cole, Asher Brown Durand, Thomas Doughty, Frederick Church—began to paint wilderness landscapes just beyond the well-settled Hudson River Valley.

Wishing to preserve the wilderness in paint before the hand of civilization erased it, they sought sublimity, beauty, and God's ordering hand in the Adirondack Mountains and the waterfalls of the Catskills. Between Cooper and Cole especially, personal relations were to be continuing, and artistic influences were to work both ways, as shown by the three paintings Cole did of scenes in *The Last of the Mohicans* (one illustrates this book's cover). As in many a Hudson River School painting, Cooper's novels repeatedly set up a character as the feeling observer of a landscape that is described in detail, either by the character or by the narrator. Cooper's words thus provide a stationary framed painting within which natural details are forever in motion. After reading many such passages in *The Pathfinder*, Balzac exclaimed, "Never did typographed language approach so closely to painting. This is the school that literary landscape-painters ought to study; all the secrets of the art are here" (197).

Within this context, let us consider how Cooper renders Hawkeye's ecstatic description of Glenn's Falls. Seeking safety from an attack by Magua and his Hurons, Duncan Heyward, David Gamut, and Alice and Cora Munro have been led by Leatherstocking, Chingachgook, and Uncas to a cavern behind and between a doubly cascading waterfall. Hawkeye, an illiterate scout who probably could never have seen a landscape painting, stands in front of the waterfall, detailing his visual responses to the framed scene:

> Ay! there are the falls on two sides of us, and the river above and below. If you had daylight, it would be worth the trouble to step up on the height of this rock, and look at the perversity of the water! It falls by no rule at all; sometimes it leaps, sometimes it tumbles; there, it skips; here, it shoots; in one place 'tis white as snow, and in another 'tis green as grass; hereabouts, it pitches into deep hollows that rumble and quake the 'arth; and thereaway, it ripples and sings like a brook, fashioning whirlpools and gullies in the old stone, as if 'twas no harder than trodden clay. The whole design of the river seems disconcerted. First it runs smoothly, as if meaning to go down the descent as things were ordered; then it angles about and faces the shores; nor are there places wanting, where it looks backward, as if unwilling to leave the wilderness,

to mingle with the salt! Ay, lady, the fine cobweb-looking cloth you wear at your throat, is coarse, and like a fish net, to little spots I can show you, where the river fabricates all sorts of images, as if, having broke loose from order, it would try its hand at every thing. And yet what does it amount to! After the water has been suffered to have its will for a time, like a headstrong man, it is gathered together by the hand that made it, and a few rods below you may see it all, flowing on steadily towards the sea, as was foreordained from the first foundation of the 'arth! (64–65)

Hawkeye's words are, first of all, a marvelous description of a waterfall. His eye descends steadily downward from the water's initial leap to its separating into cascades, its eddying at the falls' bottom, and its final runoff. The whole paragraph makes one composite picture, but inside the frame there is constant motion. As Hawkeye describes the water gathering speed, he speaks in quick gasping phrases full of active verbs ("leaps . . . tumbles . . . skips . . . shoots"). As the streams eddy into pools along the side, the rhythms of Hawkeye's words become slower and more regularly musical ("and thereaway it ripples and sings like a brook"). His excitement at so lovely a picture of nature's power and purity is conveyed not by any flat statement of his feeling but by his exclamatory slang and by the vividness of his metaphors (the pitching water "as green as grass" or the water-worn stone "no harder than trodden clay"). Only after he has described the final countercurrent does he turn to Alice Munro and pointedly insist that her green veil, already made a symbol for the finery of civilization, is "coarse" by comparison to all she is witnessing. Cooper even allows Hawkeye to express the Melvillean and Modernist belief that, for any observor, "the river fabricates all kinds of images," thereby allowing us, within limits, to see ourselves or whatever we wish in its watery visions.

As we read the passage, we become aware that Cooper, if not Hawkeye, intends a second and third layer of meaning. Hawkeye's words describe a waterfall but they also sum up the course both of an individual's life and of collective human affairs. Our lives begin in smoothness, gather energy, divide into separate currents, rest in momentary eddies, then plunge on downward. Although we thrust

ourselves momentarily against the current, thereby testing our individual energies, our separate countercurrents are all resistlessly gathered
at the end, flowing on together toward some silent sea. This allegorical
view of history and of a human life (somewhat like a "conceit" in an
Elizabethan sonnet and very like the particular "conceit" in Robert
Frost's "West-Running Brook") can and should be applied to the way
Cooper's characters act in the novel, both as individuals and as representatives of their race, nation, or social class. In particular, however,
we feel here the muted optimism of Hawkeye's outlook. Raised among
the Moravians, Hawkeye sees in the water images of Glenn's Falls the
broadly Christian—but particularly Protestant—view that the Fall of
Man is the central act in human history. But instead of insisting on
depravity, original sin or man's unconditional election to heaven and
hell, Hawkeye voices a Deistic view of life's process, leading all
onlookers toward the conclusion that, although the countercurrents of
human history are real, they are both temporary and ultimately controlled by some unnameable power. Seen from the perspective of the
sea toward which all waters flow, the individual streams have been
"foreordained" to be gathered by the unspecified "hand" that made
them. We may ripple and sing like a brook in our youth; we may
break loose from order so as to try our hand at most anything during
our first maturity; but in the end "the perversity of the water" will be
quieted into one human river (red indistinguishable from white?)
"flowing on steadily towards the sea."

In Romantic literature generally, truths observed in nature are
given far greater authority than the presumably outmoded revelations
of Scripture. The force and beauty of Hawkeye's words, together with
the admirable qualities of his character, have led many readers to
assume that Hawkeye's view of life's waterfall must also be Cooper's.
Such an assumption is, however, highly problematic. Leatherstocking
is a created character, wholly separate in origin, class, skills, and ways
of life from James Fenimore Cooper. Leatherstocking's assertion of a
hidden "hand" that controls and eventually resolves conflict is flatly
inconsistent with the view of history Cooper has introduced at his
novel's opening. The "gallant and reckless youth" who threw himself
into colonial conflict may have made his "inroads," but his "long night

of forgetfulness" is described as a solitary forest death, not a gathering back into life's universal sea. Cooper the disillusioned historian and Cooper the nature romantic seem clearly in conflict here. Perhaps Leatherstocking sees in the waterfall what Cooper wishes were true. Or perhaps Cooper would have us recognize that not even Leatherstocking could act the hero's part if he fully accepted history's violent meaninglessness.

As soon as Hawkeye finishes picturing the waterfall, Cooper remarks that "his auditors received a cheering assurance of the security of their place of concealment, from this untutored description of Glenn's" (65). Stylistically, these words are one of those remarkably awkward sentences by which Cooper makes a bridge from dialogue or description back into narrative. But they contain more than first appears. In fact, as Cooper's next chapter will show, "the cheering assurance" that Hawkeye's listeners have derived from his response to Glenn's Falls proves to be wholly illusory. Bullets and tomahawks drive the listeners back into the cave, where nearly all will be captured. While Leatherstocking has been discoursing on the waterfall of life, Magua and the Hurons have been gathering around him in hope of taking his life away. Although Cooper offers no conclusion about the danger and vanity of philosophizing, such conclusions are there to be reached.

Even more astonishing is Cooper's passing reference to Hawkeye's eloquence as an "untutored description of Glenn's." No landscape painting could be more vivid or more rich in meaning, yet Cooper seems to slight Hawkeye's speech by summarily judging it as unschooled. The second edition of the *Oxford English Dictionary*, however, lists synonyms of wide-ranging connotations for the word *untutored*: "uneducated, untaught; simple, unsophisticated; rude, boorish." Can we be sure that to James Fenimore Cooper the word *untutored* did not imply "free of artifical literary sophistication" rather than "rudely uneducated"? Or was Cooper so concerned about retaining the authority of his own gentlemanly English that he wanted to make sure his reader knew that Hawkeye's slang is a sign of a boorish scout's lack of education? We can reach only two firm conclusions. First, in 1826 *untutored* was one of those words that were absorbing the conflicting values of the Age of Reason and the Age of Romanticism. Second, the sentence in which Cooper appears to discredit Hawkeye's words unintentionally shows that Hawkeye's slang, like Huckleberry Finn's, can be more expressive than the stylistic proprieties of formal education.

After Leatherstocking concludes his speech on Glenn's Falls, three chapters of varied battle and adventure narrative follow. Before the sequence ends with Magua carrying the Munro sisters into captivity, Cooper describes two climactic hand-to-hand battles, both of them between a white man and an Indian. These combats, which conclude chapter 7, are described in parallel narrative within one immensely long (and here abridged) paragraph:

> With ready skill, Hawk-eye and his antagonist each grasped the uplifted arm of the other, which held the dangerous knife. For near a minute, they stood looking one another in the eye, and gradually exerting the power of their muscles for the mastery. At length, the toughened sinews of the white man prevailed over the less practised limbs of the native. The arm of the Indian slowly gave way before the increasing force of the scout, who suddenly wresting his armed hand from the grasp of his foe, drove the sharp weapon through his naked bosom to the heart. In the meantime, Heyward had been pressed in a more deadly struggle . . . as to who should cast the other over the dizzy height into a neighbouring cavern of the falls. Every successive struggle brought them nearer to the verge, where Duncan perceived the final and conquering effort must be made. Each of the combatants threw all his energies into that effort and the result was, that both tottered on the brink of the precipice. Heyward felt the grasp of the other at his throat, and saw the grim smile the savage gave, under the revengeful hope that he hurried his enemy to a fate similar to his own, as he felt his body slowly yielding to a resistless power, and the young man experienced the passing agony of such a moment in all its horrors. At that instant of extreme danger, a dark hand and glancing knife appeared before him; the Indian released his hold, as the blood flowed freely from around the severed tendons of his wrist; and while Duncan was drawn backward by the saving arm of Uncas, his charmed eyes were still riveted on the fierce and

disappointed countenance of his foe, who fell sullenly and disappointed down the irrecoverable precipice. (81–82)

Anyone who has grown up within American society has seen or read both of these fights at least a hundred times, whether in adventure serials, in John Ford's films, in countless B westerns, in the James Bond books and films, in *Star Wars*, in *Indiana Jones and the Temple of Doom*, or in fiction by Jack London or Ernest Hemingway or Norman Mailer. We may be asked to visualize arm-wrestlers in a bar, a matador and a bull, a six-gun duel in the middle of Main Street, laser-wielding knights on the edges of space, or suave secret agents atop a Riviera casino, but all of these are variants on one scene that seems to have timeless appeal, at least to a male audience. In Western literature, the ultimate source of them all is the single combat between Hector and Achilles in the *Iliad*, but in twentieth-century American culture, the immediate and clearly prototypical source can be found in the foregoing passage from *The Last of the Mohicans*.

Why has this kind of conflict, with all its variants, proved to be so endlessly satisfying? The essence of the appeal is the climactic defeat of a villain, representing some kind of "other," who is confronted either on a dramatically visualized precipice (cliff, casino, or spacecraft) or in the midst of a circle of onlookers (bar, bullring, or Main Street). Even if the paradigm seems crude because it has been so overworked, Cooper's passage shows us subtleties of technique that can still provide satisfaction. The victories of Leatherstocking and Heyward are total, but the fights are long protracted so as to enhance the final release. We see the bodies of the two pairs of combatants in a kind of slow-motion freeze frame, the red and white skins locked into the spending of almost equal force against each another. Hawkeye, who combines red forest skills with white strength, overcomes his assailant by his own effort. Duncan Heyward, however, who has no experience of the forest or the Indian, must be saved from red villainy in a last second rescue by a red hero. Both combats end in a conclusive, cleanly delivered blow (a knife into the heart, blood flowing over severed wrist tendons) that is then immediately forgotten. The vanquished red foe, who is kept conveniently nameless, is erased from memory as he falls from sight over the precipice that had made him important. The lengthy sentences and compound phrases lend the entire passage a dreamlike, fevered, and abstract quality. Like the measured tones of today's television newscaster, Cooper's prose describes irrational horrors in controlled phrases, measured tones, and proper sentences. His too is a medium trying to control the recurrent senselessness of its message.

Mark Twain's "Fenimore Cooper's Literary Offenses" (1895) ridicules the inaccuracies of Cooper's prose style every bit as aggressively as it does the absurdities of Leatherstocking's feats of derring-do. Sure that good realistic fiction avoids abstract words and long sentences, Twain pretends that Cooper violated 18 of the 19 rules of literary art, half of which pertain to matters of style. Cooper's characters, Twain says, speak in stilted dialogue that does not even "sound like human talk" (277). When Cooper attempts to describe something, his abstract language defeats him. "Cooper's eye was splendidly inaccurate," Twain contends: "Cooper seldom saw anything correctly. He saw nearly all things as through a glass eye, darkly" (280). Accusing Cooper of "literary sharping and flatting," Twain even provided a list of 34 words Cooper presumably misused in six pages of *The Deerslayer*, together with their presumably correct alternatives (286). The final 7 rules Cooper has violated are "12. Say what he [the author] is proposing to say, not merely come near it. 13. Use the right word, not its second cousin. 14. Eschew surplusage. 15. Not omit necessary details. 16. Avoid slovenliness of form. 17. Use good grammar. 18. Employ a simple and straightforward style" (278). At essay's end, Twain observes that "there have been daring people in the world who claimed that Cooper could write English, but they are all dead now" (286)—except, that is, for a few professors who are themselves among the walking dead, unable to perceive that *The Deerslayer* is "not a work of art in any sense, . . . just simply a literary *delerium tremens*" (286).

Hilarious though Twain's essay is, it is valid only within its own narrow and sometimes misapplied criteria. Whether Twain is attacking Cooper's diction or Hawkeye's tracking feats, his strategy is to charge Cooper with one small inaccuracy, reconstruct the surrounding narrative or sentence around it, and then produce the whole as evidence that Cooper's kind of English would prevent anyone from seeing reality. In the three passages we have considered, it is not hard to find instances of faulty or inconsistent diction. Even Hawkeye, for example, sounds something like a half-dead professor when he observes that "the whole design of the river seems disconcerted" (64). And yet when read in context, these kinds of failings do not destroy or even appreciably lessen the power of the whole passage. "A work of art," Twain's denial notwithstanding, is exactly what *The Last of the Mohicans* is. Moroever, Twain had read Cooper more extensively than his relentless mockery would suggest; while enumerating Cooper's offenses, Twain selects details from three of the Leatherstocking tales. In defense of Cooper's elaborate style, it may even be argued that his measured sentences enhance one effect even more pertinent to our times than to his. Rendering the bloody violence of the frontier through the prose medium of an eighteenth-century gentleman shows a deep cultural need to control unreason through reason. Cooper's prose, we may say, sometimes seems as out of place as red- and blue-coated European troops trying to march through a New World's wilderness. Such discontinuities, we come to feel, are as absurd as they are dangerous.

GENRE

"To understand any object, we first must know to what category of things it belongs." Ever since Aristotle wrote *Of Poetry* (about 330 B.C.), critics and readers who agree with this proposition have been interested in defining the various kinds—genres—of literature by dividing broad categories (e.g., poetry, fiction, drama, and essay) into subdivisions in order to define the qualities that belong to each. There is, however, an equally plausible counterproposition, which may be phrased as follows: "To understand any object, we first must know it on its own terms, without regard to preexisting categories." Ever since Longinus wrote *On the Sublime* (about A.D. 100), many critics and most readers have been interested in the intrinsic formal and stylistic qualities of a particular text without worrying overmuch about the classification to which it belongs. Because all readers, including Aristotle and Longinus, have laid claim to both positions when appropriate or convenient, the determining of genre takes place within a spectrum of shades between absolute deductive reasoning ("*Hamlet* is a tragedy and therefore has these qualities") and absolute inductive reasoning ("*Hamlet* has these particular qualities that it shares with no other work we call a tragedy"). Study of the genre of a single work can be no more valid than the general definitions of kind it employs. Genre study must always to some degree distort the individual text, but broad and useful comparisons among texts have proved almost impossible without it.

The Last of the Mohicans was written at a time when long-standing categories of genre had recently been broken down and redefined. In the late seventeenth and early eighteenth centuries, the so-called neoclassical critics had attempted to arrange literature in a timeless hierarchy of universal kinds. Owing to the cultural upheavals caused by the American and French Revolutions, these kinds of categorizing had come to seem increasingly barren and confining. The distinction between history (a narrative of true events in the distant past) and the novel (a narrative of made-up events in the near present) had been broken down first by Henry Fielding (*The History of Tom Jones*, 1749) and, even more spectacularly, by Walter Scott through his invention of the historical novel. The epic poem, long revered as the highest genre of all, was clearly dying out, being replaced by new kinds of heroic literature in prose as well as poetry. The supposed separation between two kinds of narrative poetry, the classical heroic "epic" and the medieval chivalric "romance," was disappearing into new kinds of unclassifiable poems as different as Scott's *The Lay of the Last Minstrel*, Coleridge's "The Rhyme of the Ancient Mariner," Byron's *Don Juan*, and Keats's "Lamia." Even the literary boundaries of prose and poetry were dissolving as the ever-increasing popularity of prose assimilated older poetic forms. Medieval romance was absorbed into the Gothic novel, heroic poetry into prose narrative, and the formal elegy into prose lamention for lost races.

Scott's historical novel, the genre to which *The Last of the Mohicans* most clearly belongs, was itself a hybrid of history and fiction, romance and novel, cultivated sentiment and social description, the epic and the elegy. Its essence, as the great Hungarian critic Georg Lukacs perceived, was to follow the changing fortunes of an intelligent but rather ordinary gentleman in times of rebellion or revolution. This protagonist is almost always a waverer between opposed historical forces representing the Old Order (medieval, Catholic, and aristocratic) and the New Order (futuristic, Protestant, and republican). Fictional characters are placed in realistically described historical settings. The narrative propels the characters toward an important historical conflict (usually a battle) that forces the wavering hero through crises of allegiance. Famous historical figures (Bonnie Prince Charlie, Catherine the Great, Napoleon, George Washington, etc.), embodying historical forces in concentrated form, make brief but climactic appearances. As Lukacs observed, the first generation of historical novelists wrote with a new and acute sense of historical change emerging from the immense losses and gains of the French and American Revolutions. Thus, Scott's wavering heroes deeply engaged the reader's uncertainty and worry about entering into an increasingly international, republican, and capitalistic world where individuals were freer to think and to define themselves beyond the confines of old regional or tribal loyalties.

In 1820, America was still a comparatively isolated nation, advanced in its republican polity but decidedly preindustrial and backed by an immense frontier. For Cooper, the conflicting attractions of regressive regional cultures and progressive nationalism had to be presented in a context different from Scott's. Accordingly, *The Last of the Mohicans* imitates yet changes Scott's kind of historical fiction. The center of Cooper's narrative, the event toward which and from which the fictive plot moves, is the British surrender of Fort William Henry to the French and the infamous "massacre" that immediately followed. Like Scott, Cooper makes us feel that fictional characters are half-knowingly caught up in real historical forces much greater than themselves. The commander of the French Army, the Marquis de Montcalm, embodies exactly the kinds of feudal, aristocratic, and

Catholic forces that, to self-conscious republicans like Cooper, formed the collective blocking force to progress. At novel's end, Cooper's officer-protagonist, the Virginia-born Lieutenant Duncan Heyward, marries the fair-haired and genteel Alice Munro, very much as Scott's Lieutenant Edward Waverley marries Rose Bradwardine after the Battle of Culloden. In both novels, as in much nineteenth-century western thought, the Protestant gentleman of good will and considerable means prevails as the social force of the future.

In less fortunate ways too, Walter Scott's influence is evident. The psalmodist David Gamut, like many of Scott's "humor" characters, is a talkative eccentric whose single obsession and dialect humor grow increasingly tiresome. At times we feel that, like most historical novels, *The Last of the Mohicans* contains too many characters, too much description, too involved a plot. A lighter touch would sometimes be welcome in the narrative voice, instead of the portentous tone that Scott himself mocked as the "big bow-wow strain" in his fiction.[4]

Because the war between the French and English armies occupies the foreground of the novel's conflict, it is easy to assume that the Protestant English, like Scott's mercantile Hanoverians, represent the New Order whereas the Catholic French, like Scott's agricultural Highlanders, represent the Old. The only character at all concerned to make such a distinction, however, is Hawkeye, whose comic prejudices against the French are self-evident. In other ways, as the opening paragraphs suggest, there is little real distinction between the opposed armies, both of which are imperial and aristocratic. Lieutenant Colonel Munro, commander of the British forces at the fort, is himself a Scot whose love of feudal allegiance and traditional military codes turns out to be far more honorable in practice than Montcalm's aristocratic pretense, but not more progressive in kind. As we become immersed in Cooper's narrative, the supposed distinctions between French and English gradually blur and then drop away, while the conflict between the red and white cultures grows ever more important. The true ancien régime in Cooper's novel turns out to be the traditional hunting and warrior culture of the North American Indian, whereas the future is embodied in the literate, property-owning whites (French, English, or colonials) who are dispossessing them. As George Sand observed, the genuine and historically lasting conflict of values in Cooper's Leatherstocking novels is racial. The power of *The Last of the Mohicans* thus depends on Cooper's appreciation for the integrity of Indian culture, just as *Waverley*'s power derives from Scott's appreciation for the bravery of the Highlander. For Scott, the conflict of the Old and New orders was finally, however, a matter of conflicting national cultures. When Cooper placed race at the center of the historical novel, he redrew the lines of Old and New in a way that was simultaneously behind and ahead of the kinds of conflicts that marked post–Napoleonic Europe.

Scott's Edward Waverley vacillates between his duties as an officer in the Hanoverian Army and his attraction to the loyalties and traditions of the Highland clan. Cooper, however, allows no wavering between national allegiances within his white characters. Hawkeye is conceived, it is true, as an amalgamation of the best qualities of Indian and white cultures. Consequently, he is as critical of the white man's law court as he is of the red man's torture stake—and he sees similarities between them. In Hawkeye's view, the white men's books get no closer to God's truth than the Red Man's council songs. But Hawkeye does not, like Waverley, join first one group and then the other, returning luckily to the winning cause at novel's end. Instead, we see Hawkeye, from the first, as a protagonist who has already made a decision to live between the Old and the New, belonging to neither. The issue, then, is not one of forming an ethically defensible national allegiance that allows for a possibly better future. It is, rather, a question of sheer survival for all of those groups—Hurons, Iroquois, Delawares, Mohicans, French, English, the colonists, and Hawkeye—whose allegiances are already formed but whose territorial boundaries are insecure. As we shall see, Hawkeye is deeply troubled by the question of how a Christian white man should act in a wilderness where retaliatory codes of Indian warfare, or none at all, prevail. But Hawkeye forever insists that, despite his Indian ways and Mohican friends, he remains in essence a white man, a "man without a cross" who, though he will serve the English army on occasion, will also refuse to live within white civilization.

The shift Cooper has here made in Scott's model of a wavering hero has enormous consequences. Like Scott, Cooper believes that conflict between worthy and opposed historical forces is inevitable. In Cooper's world, however, changing one's allegiance, undergoing a conversion of inner values, is neither a common nor a genuine experience. In the face of all the cliché's about the openness of the New World, Cooper places us in a dense forest where individual free will, if it exists, does not result in inner change. In this sense, the "republican" Cooper has a sense of fatality that is, ironically, at least equal to that of the "tory" Scott.

After Scott published *Ivanhoe* (1820), writers of historical fiction imitated and inorporated so many of the conventions of romance that the phrase "historical romance" would long become almost as common a designation as "historical novel." Throughout the nineteenth century, the term romance became associated with a kind of fiction that was removed or exotic in setting, archetypal in characterization, sensational or suspenseful in plot, and melodramatic in tone. For good reason, these romance qualities are exactly those associated with *The Last of the Mohicans*, even by those who have not read it. At its most elementary level, Cooper's plot provides ever new ways of making readers wonder whether two beautiful maidens will get through the dark forest, escape torture by a band of vengeful Indians, and be reclaimed from a captivity that threatens rape as well as death. Nevertheless, Cooper's novel is also a romance in the more complex sense in which twentieth-century critics of fiction have used that term—a kind of fiction concerned with psychological and psychohistorical issues and feelings that transcend the matters of money, class, and marriage arising in more ordinary communities described in novels of manners. In this sense, Hawkeye, Magua, and Cora all acquire a depth and complexity far beyond the charge of two-dimensional characterization often leveled at the romance.

Two other ways in which Cooper's novel clearly was designed as a romance deserve special consideration. Duncan Heyward's constant concern for the safety of Alice and Cora Munro is a fictional variant of the medieval romance of chivalry, in which a knight both protects his lady and engages in a quest on her behalf. Cooper uses this motif both to initiate and to sustain his plot, but he does not affirm it in any simple-minded way. Duncan Heyward's expressions of concern for Alice are as exaggerated as Alice's protestations of helplessness. Not only is Duncan Heyward an abysmal failure as Alice's protector-knight; Cooper makes it plain that Heyward is playacting, trying to live out a role internalized from his reading. Determined to maintain nightwatch because he has fallen asleep on guard the day before, Heyward once more "sunk into a deep sleep, dreaming that he was a knight of ancient chivalry, holding his midnight vigils before the tent of a re-captured princess, whose favour he did not despair of gaining, by such a proof of devotion and watchfulness" (147). Ironically, the Munro sisters can be effectively protected by Leatherstocking and the Mohicans, but not by the handsome lieutenant. Insofar as chivalry remains at all pertinent to survival in the American forest, it exists in the silent service that Uncas tenderly extends to Cora, not in the wordy protestations of the white gentleman toward fair-haired Alice.

In his second preface to the novel, Cooper insisted that "the business of a writer of fiction is to approach, as near as his powers will allow, to poetry" (9–10). By the time he completed the Leatherstocking series, the writing of poetic prose was to seem the very essence of fictive romance. The 1850 preface ends with the following paragraph:

> It is the privilege of all writers of fiction, more particularly when their works aspire to the elevation of romances, to present the *beau-ideal* of their characters to the reader. This it is which constitutes poetry, and to suppose that the red man is to be represented only in the squalid misery or in the degraded moral state that certainly more or less belongs to his condition is, we apprehend, taking a very narrow view of an author's privileges. Such criticism would have deprived the world of even Homer. (398)

In this crucial paragraph, the word *romance* suggests "poetry," and poetry" in turn suggests the Indian. The element of romance in the Leatherstocking Tales is thus associated not with plotting out chivalrous deeds amid forest dangers, but with portraying the undegraded moral state of the Indian (the *beau-ideal* of Indian character) directly to the reader.

Perceiving romance in Indian character involves, as we shall see, many separate things, but perhaps the romancer's essential challenge is to create a poetic language of seeming authenticity. Cooper assumes, as we do today, that because the Indian has lived a more natural life than the white man, the Indian must speak a more natural language. The speech of Cooper's red men is thus authentic only in the restricted sense that it derives from a defensible premise about the Indian's natural life. Instead of attempting to master and translate Indian languages, which would have been possible, though difficult, in the 1820s, Cooper invents for his Indians a language he believes to be natural and therefore appropriate for romance. The Indian, he argues, "draws his metaphors from the clouds, the seasons, the birds, the beasts and the vegetable world" (7). Language based on natural metaphors, rather than the white man's abstractions, is not, however, any less accurate. In fact, the poetry of Indian speech may penetrate to deeper truths. "The imagery of the Indian," Cooper surmises, is "chastened and perhaps improved, by the limited range of his practical knowledge" (7).

The language of natural metaphor, then, is a language of romance as well as historical truth, even though it is no longer a language of social power. Consider Chingachgook's rendering of the Mohicans' memory of their tribal origin:

> We come from the place where the sun is hid at night, over great plains where the buffaloes live, until we reached the big river. There we fought the Alligewi, till the ground was red with their blood. From the banks of the big river to the shores of the salt lake, there was none to meet us. The Maquas followed at a distance. . . . Then, Hawk-eye, we were one people, and we were happy. The salt lake gave us its fish, the woods its deer, and the air its birds. We took wives who bore us children; we worshipped the Great Spirit; and we kept the Maquas beyond the sound of our songs of triumph. (38–39)

43

This account is not appreciably different from present anthropological record. Adapting Chingachgook's natural metaphors to contemporary prose, we find that the Mohegans (an Algonquin tribe) came from the far west, presumably down the Bering Strait and Mackenzie Corridor, confronted the Mound Builders at the Mississippi River, and then settled along the Atlantic shore, keeping the Maquas (Mohawks—Iroquois) at proper territorial distance. Chingachgook makes it clear that the Mohicans moved seasonally, following coastal food sources in—as we would say—an ecologically balanced lifestyle. He sadly admits, however, that the time of Algonquin unity and Mohican happiness is now over because, as we learn in the next paragraph, Dutchmen and Englishmen, who knew how to divide by conquering, came upon Mohegan land with their firewater and paper land claims. Chingachgook's natural metaphors are, of course, entirely of Cooper's making, but are they therefore "fake"? And whose account makes more memorable reading, Chingachgook's metaphoric prose-poetry or my clunky polysyllabic abstractions?

Writing romance induces novelists to create characters who typify good and evil, as Cooper's split view of the Indian suggests. In fashioning a plot for his novel, Cooper freely adapted another genre that also relies on a good-evil, black-white view of human character—the Captivity Narrative. Captivity Narratives began to be published immediately after the devastation of King Philip's War (1675–76), a massive uprising of the remaining tribes in New England that killed 10 percent of the region's adult white male population and checked frontier expansion for some 50 years. Amid a Puritan culture deeply suspicious of fiction, the Captivity Narrative allowed an outlet for the imagination to flourish within the survivor's recounting of his or her harrowing wilderness experience. Often reprinted and imitated, the captivity narratives of Mary Rowlandson and John Williams, together with those told to Cotton Mather, established a set of conventions that were to be popularly and profitably reworked until the 1840s. The captivity narrative was a survivor account, often written by a mother who recalls how brutal savages abruptly devastated her peaceful Christian settlement, killing members of her family, burning buildings and crops, and then carrying off prominent survivors for purposes of revenge or ransom. The writer then recounts a harrowing journey through the wilderness, in which she confronts starvation, sickness, forced labor, the death of children, and the threat of torture, or, much more rarely, of rape. The earlier Captivity Narratives ended, however, in the triumph of release, as the captive is restored to civilization and thankfully reunited with his or her own people.

At its best, the Captivity Narrative provided a genuine test of Puritan spiritual belief. The writer, who has thought of herself as a worthy Christian, wonders whether God has let the red savages loose upon her family as a punishment either for her sins, for the sins of the community, or for reasons unknowable. The experience of captivity then becomes God's prolonged trial of faith, a "merciful affliction," through which the sufferer learns that she can trust in no earthly security. At its worst, however, the Captivity Narrative became a sensationalist vehicle for releasing fear and hatred for Indians, Catholics, and Frenchmen: the final "deliverance" or "redemption" of the Captive was assumed to be God's way of pointing out His righteous remnant. By 1757—when the hold of Puritan spirituality was markedly lessening, when the French-English struggle was at its height, and the urge to dispossess the Indian was continuing to gather force—the Captivity Narrative became increasingly secular and even more abusive because its racism was now primarily based on ethnic rather than religious distinctions.

Cooper uses the conventions of the Captivity Narrative to sustain suspense, to move his characters to and from Fort William Henry, and to bring them together at the final Delaware Council scene. Chapters 10–14, 18–26, and 31–32 repeat the same narrative sequence. Momentarily victorious through bravery as well as trickery, Magua captures Cora and Alice Munro, and leads them off into the wilderness, supposedly in order to take Cora back to the Hurons in French Canada, where she shall be forced to be his woman. Leatherstocking, Heyward, the Mohicans, and, in the last two sequences, Colonel Munro all set off to pursue and reclaim them, a mission of secular salvation in which they are never fully successful.

Although the threat of torture and rape is ever present, Cooper focuses on the excitements of the chase, and strategies of tracking and disguise, rather than ascribing degrading brutalities to the Huron captors.

The major change Cooper has made in the model of the Captivity Narrative is his insistence on a totally different motivation for the act of capture. To the Puritans, Indians had swept down on their frontier villages because they were red savages bent on killing white Christians. In Puritan Captivity Narratives, we are almost never allowed within the mind of the captors, never permitted to see anything in a captor's red face beyond a mask of willfull cruelty or brutal indifference. Magua's motive, however, is revenge for a completely unjustified brutality inflicted by a white man. By publicly whipping Magua for drunkenness (a crime made possible only by the presence of white armies), Colonel Munro has understandably driven Magua to retaliate rather than to forgive. Instead of taking revenge on Munro directly, Magua lusts to torment Munro through possessing Cora's body: "When the blows scorched the back of the Huron, he would know where to find a woman to feel the smart. The daughter of Munro would draw his water, hoe his corn, and cook his venison. The body of the gray-head would sleep among his cannon, but his heart would be within reach of the knife of le Subtil" (119). Knifing a father's heart by possessing his daughter may be the act of a subtle fox (as Magua's French epithet suggests), but there is no gainsaying that the initial, interracial wrong was done by the white father or, if one prefers, by the common practices of white conquest. Although Cooper elicits horror at abduction and impending rape, he never allows his reader to see captive women simply as victims of a causeless red malice.

David Gamut may not know why he is journeying to Fort William Henry, but Cooper has a use for his being there beyond a hopefully comic display of garrulity. As a psalmodist from Connecticut, David represents the sometimes touching but usually absurd falsities of the Puritan view of wilderness life. Gamut's belief that singing the psalms of David will persuade the Lord to protect his white companions is, in Cooper's eyes, as much an illusion as the Puritan captive's hope that carrying the Bible will provide security as well as spiritual comfort. In the face of all evidence, Gamut presumes that white Christians will practice the Sixth Commandment of God ("Thou Shalt Not Kill"). He also presumes that Indians are red heathen driven by bloodlust. Although David believes that mercy and nonviolence are white virtues, he conveniently forgets—as Leatherstocking almost never does—that white colonial powers have passed laws paying bounties for scalps. In order to try to understand his situation, David repeatedly assesses it through the outmoded pilgrimage vocabulary of the Captivity Narrative. Although he and the Munro "maidens" are now "captives to the heathen," David reluctantly admits that "though our wayfaring has been sore, and our sustenance scanty, we have had little other cause for complaint, except the violence done our feelings, by being thus led in captivity into a far land" (253). When David assumes that the Indians must be "among the profanest of the idolatrous," Hawkeye immediately rebukes him for yielding to a "wicked fabrication of the whites" who wish to "belie the nature of the Indian" (256). The ultimate irony of David Gamut's illusions is that their absurdity, not their truth, serves to protect him. When David, singing his psalms, wanders onto the middle of a battlefield, the Indians refuse to attack him because they assume he must be insane. Indian forbearance, not God's will, is the cause of his survival.

During the half-century after 1776, the writing of a great literary epic was an eagerly awaited sign of America's cultural maturity. After the failure of many imitative verse epics—like Joel Barlow's *The Columbiad* (1807)—in praise of republican civilization, more daring writers began to entertain two heretical notions. Perhaps the epic could survive if the pseudo-Homeric poem could be discarded and the essence of the epic adapted into popular genres like prose historical romance. And perhaps the great heroic subject for American writers was not the spread of white civilization across the West but the demise of those noble red peoples who had long inhabited it. The stakes here were high. Traditional educational assumptions about both literary merit and civic virtue would have to be undermined if not abandoned. White readers, proud that their literacy and their print culture placed them above the savage state, would be reading a new kind of epic literature, one suggesting that America's true heroism lay not in the civilization Europeans brought to the New World, but in the "savagery" they themselves were erasing from it.

The key to change was to convince the reader that Indians were not "idolatrous heathen," as David Gamut would have it, but the last of the known world's heroic-age peoples. A new interest in origins led writers of many persuasions to seek out cultural customs that Homer's Greeks and America's Indians seemed to have had in common: a warrior and hunting culture that valorized honor in battle, councils during which chieftains tested their eloquence, the subordination of women, elaborate rites of hospitality, and even more elaborate rites of burial. These qualities are repeatedly ascribed to Indians throughout the Leatherstocking Tales, especially in *The Last of the Mohicans*. In later years, Cooper tacitly acknowledged his ambition to write a romance-epic. Sensing the similarities between the Indians of the Leatherstocking Tales and the Scottish Highlanders of the Waverley novels, Cooper wrote in 1838 that Scott had "raised the novel, as near as might be, to the dignity of the epic."[5] The last sentence of Cooper's 1850 preface ("Such criticism would have deprived the world of even Homer"[398]) shows Cooper's desire to link Mycenaean Greeks to American Indians, and thereby to incorporate the red man's spoken poetry within the white writer's epic prose.

A defining convention of epic poetry, from Homer's *Iliad* (about 900 B.C.) through Milton's *Paradise Lost* (1667), had been a climactic single combat between heroic chieftains. The fight between Magua and Chingachgook in chapter 12 of *The Last of the Mohicans* begins with a claim upon the poetic conventions of the heroic epithet and epic simile:

> The battle was now entirely terminated, with the exception of the protracted struggle between "le Renard Subtil" and "le Gros Serpent." Well did these barbarous warriors prove that they deserved those significant names, which had been bestowed for deeds in former wars. When they engaged, some little time was lost in eluding the quick and vigorous thrusts which had been aimed at their lives. Suddenly darting on each other, they closed, and came to the earth, twisted together, like twining serpents, in pliant and subtle folds. At the moment when the victors found

themselves unoccupied, the spot where these experienced and desperate combatants lay, could only be distinguished by a cloud of dust and leaves, which moved from the centre of the little plain toward its boundary, as if raised by the passage of a whirl-wind. (129)

Cooper's pointed recall of epic conventions here coexists with his uneasy use of them. Although he evidently desires to elevate the hero-ism of the two warriors, he continues to call them "barbarous." The epic simile he uses, however appropriate it may be visually, reduces the admirable as well as the treacherous Indian to mutually indistinguish-able serpents. After we are given a close-up of snakelike figures cov-ered with dust and blood, Cooper suddenly draws the viewer's eye back, reducing the combat to "a cloud of dust and leaves." Just like the epic combats of Hector and Achilles, Turnus and Aeneas, warrior spec-tators hover around to watch a heroic struggle, but in Cooper's world there is no overlooking deity. The battle in fact ends with a subtle undermining of epic convention. After Chingachgook subdues Magua with a knife thrust, Hawkeye simply cannot resist a lengthy outcry of triumph; his boast about his friend's battle prowess ironically allows Magua an opportunity to slither away uninjured.

The unease Cooper feels in scenes valorizing warfare disappears entirely, however, in scenes that describe rituals of mourning. As in the concluding book of the *Iliad*, *The Last of the Mohicans* ends with a sequence of elegiac speeches—by the Delaware women, Ultawa, David Gamut, Munro, Chingachgook, Hawkeye, and Tamenund, all of whom convey what the deaths of Cora and Uncas signify from their several viewpoints. The speeches have a collective dignity and reso-nance far beyond anything in previous American fiction. It is perfectly true, as critics have pointed out, that some of these speeches make the demise of red culture seem inevitably past even though it was still his-torically in process. Moreover, Cooper's sequencing of the speeches, beginning with the Delaware maidens and ending with an aged chief-tain, is wholly patriarchal in its priorities. But it is also true that the speeches are so eloquently written, so wholly in character for each speaker, that they attain the high elegiac effect that occurs only at the moment when tragedy and epic join. Throughout the final speeches of Chingachgook, Leatherstocking, and Tamenund, it is, after all, the Indian—in all the dignity of his fading cultural history—who is being remembered and mourned.

The bond between the Big Serpent and Hawkeye, formed over the body of Uncas and beyond the inroads of civilization, is based on total honesty, a mastery of forest skills, and an often silent sense of the divinity of nature. Hawkeye's clasping of Chingachgook's hand ("The boy has left us, Sagamore, but you are not alone" [394]) is the moment that makes their copresence and coaction possible in the four other tales. In the moment of Uncas's death, Hawkeye has lost his adopted son; in their union, Chingachgook and Leatherstocking have become surrogate sons and surrogate fathers to each other. And yet their bonding is culturally barren, both because it can yield no children and because the two men fully belong to neither red nor white culture.

The forming of the bond itself, we need to recognize, is a reworking of a crucial motif common to most epics in Western literature. The Big Serpent and Hawkeye, like many a semidivine pair of warriors in oral epic poetry (Gilgamesh and Enkidu, Achilles and Patroklos, Beowulf and Wiglanf, Roland and Oliver), can do almost everything except escape suffering and death. In Cooper's recasting of epic tradition, however, the heroic pair represent no community, have no issue and remain quite simply the last of their kind. In the Leatherstocking tales, as in *Gilgamesh*, the title hero forms his bond with a dark-skinned hunter from the wilderness; Gilgamesh and Enkidu, like Chingachgook and Hawkeye, leave civilization to undertake a series of adventurous tasks together. The outcome of their deeds is, however, utterly different. Whereas Gilgamesh ultimately returns to Uruk to defend the city walls he has built, Leatherstocking's heroic stature cannot be separated from his repeated rejections of civilization. His higher value, a joining of hand and heart with one Indian, represents a promise that, in Cooper's view, will clearly have no cultural fulfillment.

If we reduce the narrative of *The Last of The Mohicans* to its essential structure, we can see more clearly how Cooper has combined these many genres into one. For the first American edition,

Style and Genre

Cooper shaped his narrative in ways exactly suited to publication in two volumes:

Volume 1

1. Exposition (chapters 1–4)	History and historical novel
2. Battle at Glenn's Falls (5–9)	Epic and adventure-romance
3. Capture of Munro sisters (10–14)	Captivity narrative
4. Fall of Fort William Henry (15–17)	History and historical novel

Volume 2

5. Recapture of Munro sisters (18–22)	Captivity narrative
6. Rescues of Alice, Uncas, and Cora (23–30)	Adventure-romance
7. Battle of Delawares and Hurons; Deaths of Uncas and Magua (31–32)	Epic and history / Romance & captivity narrative
8. Denoument: Funeral Ceremonies (33)	Epic

As a carefully constructed hybrid of genres, *The Last of the Mohicans* gains more than it loses. Awkward transitions in tone and improbabilities of plot arise, but so do an unusual fullness of information and a richness of varying perspectives. In characterizing Magua, for example, Cooper sees him as a wronged victim (the historical-military perspective), as a heathen villain (the captivity narrative), as an elusive seducer (the romance), as a heroically defiant Satan (the epic), and, collectively, as an embodiment of "savagery" rather than "civilization" (a contemporary cultural attitude). Such plenitude makes any character, even one as fabricated from literature as Magua, seem rounded, memorable, and significant.

5

Race and Gender

To white Americans of the early national era, the Indian was a more unknown, more troubling, and even more important figure than today. In 1790, more than 2 million Indians—more than half the white population—lived west of the frontier line beyond the Allegheny Mountains. The Indian was regarded as the blocking force to further western settlement, yet white people knew that Indians had inhabited the continent long before their own arrival. In the view of nearly all Euro-Americans, Indians represented an inferior and anterior stage of human development. Hunters and warriors were regarded as nomads who could neither raise crops, treat women decently, sustain families, nor develop government. Compared to a legal deed, tribal habitation was denigrated as an unstable if not invalid way of possessing land. Indians, it was thought, merely lived off the land, whereas whites had the advanced intelligence required to develop it. White writers repeatedly dwelled on the Indian's illiteracy, alcoholism, and love of trinkets, because these traits made the red man seem a child who needed the protection and control of the white father. Evidence of polytheism, scalping, and torture rituals was regarded as a sign of barbarism that could not be tolerated. Behind all these oversimplified judgments lay the assumption that red culture was "savagery," white culture was "civilization," and the two could never peacefully coexist.

The solution? A few whites, mostly missionaries, believed that, because all men are descendants of Adam, it is the white man's duty to redeem the savage by converting him to Christianity, thus giving his soul a chance for salvation. Many more whites, mostly Jeffersonians, believed that, because all men are created equal, it is the white government's duty to reclaim the Indian by changing him from a nomadic hunter into a settled farmer whose children would learn white ways in local schools. But still more whites became convinced that the Indian either could not or would not assimilate. Within this fatalistic majority, some writers argued that the Indian should at least be protected— and, of course, gotten out of the white man's way—by being forcibly removed to lands ever farther west. Others argued that the Indian would have to be killed to make way for civilization. "Civilization or death to all American savages" first became a popular military toast during the Revolutionary War.[6] Shortly after the Civil War, U.S. Cavalry General Philip Sheridan made a passing observation that would soon be compressed into the most savage of white American sayings: "The only good Indian is a dead Indian."[7]

To see the Indians as a heroic-age people dispossessed of their lands and worthy of literary epic was an implicit challenge to all these attitudes. No one doubted that Indian wars would continue, but there was no agreement about their purpose, effect, or justification. Missionaries or Jeffersonians, who criticized the use of white military force, nonetheless saw Indian resistance to white settlement as sad folly, not heroism. Many white Indian traders, military men, and politicians realized that Indian retaliation had the advantage of increasing white prejudice. Frontier families feared Indian attack as the onset of a cruel savagery that threatened their property and their lives. In the Leatherstocking Tales, however, Indian resistance becomes potentially heroic because white wrongs are insisted upon, while Indian ways of life are accorded a value of their own. Cooper shows us all those acts of warfare which presumably prove Indian barbarism (attack from ambush, scalping, torture), but again and again Leatherstocking proclaims that these practices are an Indian's "gift"—that is, a traditional custom natural to the red race. Cooper is certainly not what we today call a multiculturalist (multiculturalism would have seemed impossible and irrational in 1820), but Cooper often writes as a cultural relativist well aware that the judgments one race passes on another are usually ethnocentric.

For his novel's epigraph, Cooper chose the plea of the Prince of Morocco to Portia in Shakespeare's *The Merchant of Venice*: "Mislike me not for my complexion / The shadowed livery of the burnished sun" (2.1.1–2). Morocco, whom the stage directions describe as a "tawny Moor dressed all in white," warns "fair Portia" not to condemn him for his skin color and thereby deny his inner valor. Morocco's words anticipate the sexual attraction between Uncas and Cora, but they also prompt the reader to question—much as Shylock will—all kinds of racial labels. Through the force of five chapter epigraphs chosen from *The Merchant of Venice*, Shylock comes to exemplify, for Cooper's reader, the likely human response to racial prejudice, whether directed toward Moors, Mohicans, or Jews. An angry victim of ethnic as well as religious slurs, Shylock demands vengeance even at the price of substantiating the prejudices against him: he exacts a pound of flesh to release a "Christian" merchant from an otherwise unpayable debt. Like Shylock, Cooper's Indians regard retaliation, not forgiveness, as the proper response to injury. The novel and the play ask their presumably white and Christian audiences whether retaliation is justifiable, and if so, under what circumstances and to what degree? Is the Indian, to whom God apparently forgot to give the New Testament, to be denigrated like a Jew or a Moroccan because he does not love his enemy or turn the other cheek?

Cooper's Indians have long been considered to be of two types: (a) "the good Indian," Nature's Roman, handsome and honest, courteous and skilled, or (b) "the bad Indian," Satan of the forest, dark-eyed and deceitful, murderous yet greatly skilled. Behind this simple, stark contrast lie eighteenth-century models of the Indian as noble savage or heathen barbarian, an equally split, symbiotic view of the Indian as the white man's "other." Only in the most general terms do these opposed images apply to Cooper's characterization of the Algonquins versus the Iroquois, the Mohicans versus the Hurons, Uncas versus Magua. To be

sure, Cooper uses this contrast to drive his plot, again and again picturing a few Mohicans or Delawares outnumbered by surrounding
Hurons or Iroquois who first threaten attack and then deliver it. But it
would be a mistake to assume that conveniences of plot determine
Cooper's view of racial identity. Opposition among red nations and
tribes, as he knew and we shall see, had repeatedly shifted in historically revealing ways. The battle practices of the "good" and "bad"
Indians in the novel itself are in fact not so different as they first seem.
When closely examined, the contrast between evil Iroquois and good
Delawares is mainly a rhetorical prejudice of Hawkeye, who repeatedly steels his own battle courage by calling his Iroquois attacker a
"skulkin' varmint," "reptyle," or "hell-hound." Although it is true that
the word *savage* is applied at least 53 times to the Iroquois and only
twice to the Delaware, it is Natty Bumppo, not Cooper, who is most
fond of the term. Most important, the categories of "good" and "bad"
Indian are much too simplistic to describe the complexity of the Indian
figures in the novel, especially of the two Mohicans and Magua.

Cooper first describes Uncas as a full-blooded "young warrior"
who stands with such a "free air and proud carriage," such "high
haughty features, pure in their native red," that he ironically seems less
a North American Indian than a classical sculpture, a "precious relic of
the Grecian chisel" (61–62). His simple clothing, graceful movements,
and "fearless eye" are all signs of a person of "no concealment," someone who would never "willingly devote his rich natural gifts to the
purpose of wanton treachery." Uncas has "all the finest proportions of
a noble head," a nobility earned because he courageously exposes his
forehead "bared to the generous scalping tuft" (62). By paragraph's
end, Heyward and the Munro sisters are described as lost in admiration of Uncas. They see him, however, not as the last of the Mohicans
but as a universalist Enlightenment ideal, "an unblemished specimen of
the noblest proportions of man" (62).

Toward his white friends and his Mohican father, Uncas acts in
exact accord with this encomium. Unlike Hawkeye, Uncas rescues
them from repeated death without ever making them ashamed of their
need for help. The silent admiration Uncas feels for Cora and the courtesy he shows to Alice may seem implausibly chivalric, but they are due

less to racial deference than to respect for women who challenge the white man's stereotype of red identity. Uncas's braveries are not tainted by boasting. The love he and his father share is perhaps the deepest human feeling in the book; it is conveyed almost wordlessly, both by their action and by the "music of their language," "the melody . . . of their low laughter," as they quietly talk in stolen moments of seeming safety (227).

There is more to Uncas, however, than the "noble savage" who first appears posed for all viewers to appreciate. After an Oneida sniper has narrowly missed shooting Chingachgook, Uncas quietly pursues the sniper, ambushes and scalps him, then brings the bloody scalping-tuft back to camp beneath his hunting shirt. This is the same Uncas, be it remembered, who has been said to look at Alice and Cora "with a sympathy, that elevated him far above the intelligence, and advanced him probably centuries before the practices of his nation" (132). Although Duncan Heyward is revolted by the barbarity of Uncas's deed, Hawkeye promptly defends the scalping as the deserved expression of Delaware hatred for an Iroquois "sarpent" (224). Uncas remains tellingly silent while Hawkeye explains that, even though "white cunning has managed to throw the tribes into great confusion" (223), leading Indians to kill Indians, it is nonetheless natural and right for a Mohican to kill an Oneida. Heyward is not convinced, but discussion is closed and the episode ends leaving a lingering taint on all sides. Even Chingachgook, after examining the scalp, drops it "with disgust depicted in his strong features" (222), not because he believes Uncas has done wrong but because he regards a renegade Oneida as unworthy of being scalped.

Cooper does not fully explain why his two most admirable red men no longer live with the Mohican remnant among the Delawares but prefer instead to associate with Leatherstocking and occasionally to serve the British Army as scouts. Cooper does, however, emphasize the compromised position the Mohicans thus occupy among their own race. The Hurons would like nothing better than to torture Uncas, not only because Uncas is trying to rescue Cora from Magua but also because they see him as someone who has sold out to British interests. This charge recurs even among Indians of Uncas's own nation. A

Delaware warrior contends in council that, instead of welcoming Uncas, the Delaware should torture him: "It is a snake—a red-skin in the pay of the Yengeese. We keep him for the torture" (345). Uncas's right to lead the Delawares in the final battle remains suspect until he reveals that he has the turtle totem on his arm. Only such an external mark of noble lineage can then save him. Uncas dies fully reclaimed as the commanding battle chief of the Mohican-Delaware, but it is hard to deny that he has in fact been "a red-skin in the pay of the Yengeese."

In creating Chingachgook, Cooper drew on another stereotype of Indian character: the aging stoic chieftain who fights for the righteous remnant of his people. Although Mark Twain's satiric misnomer ("Chicago") is unforgettable, readers of the Leatherstocking series as a whole have usually remembered Chingachgook primarily as a figure of pathos: the last survivor filled with melancholy pride in his Mohican ancestry or the drunken old man marginalized from a white frontier town. In *The Last of the Mohicans*, however, Cooper never allows Chingachgook to elicit easy sympathy. The words that first picture him are "His body, which was nearly naked, presented a terrific emblem of death, drawn in intermingled colours of white and black" (35). In the narrative that follows, Chingachgook will kill swiftly, brutally, and often. He is called the Big Serpent not only because he is wise, but because he kills with silent suddenness. Leatherstocking gives us a double explanation for the name: "not that Chingachgook, which signifies big sarpent, is really a snake, big or little; but that he understands the windings and turnings of human natur', and is silent, and strikes his enemies when they least expect him" (67). However courteous Chingachgook may be toward Delaware women and white women, he is, like Magua, proud of his abuse of his enemies' women and children: "Let the Mingo women go weep over their slain! . . . The great snake of the Mohicans has coiled himself in their wigwams and has poisoned their triumph with the wailings of children, whose fathers have not returned" (89).

The melancholy, stoic chief thus turns out to be an "emblem of death" in deed. For Chingachgook, as for everyone else who fights in these colonial wars, the price of heroism is a bloody violence that demands a hardened heart. During the dangerous approach to Fort William Henry, Hawkeye and Heyward dupe a trusting French sentinel, slipping safely by with a mixture of shadowy bravado and mumbled French. Without any tactical justification, Chingachgook promptly and wordlessly murders the sentinel, returning with the "reeking scalp of the unfortunate young Frenchman," which he displays "with the air of a man who believed he had done a deed of merit" (156). Even Hawkeye is troubled by such callousness: "Twould have been a cruel and an unhuman act for a white-skin; but 'tis the gift and natur' of an Indian, and I suppose it should not be denied! I could wish, though, it had befallen an accursed Mingo, rather than that gay, young boy, from the old countries" (156). Although Hawkeye's cultural relativism here compels him to be reconciled to scalping as an Indian custom, he cannot hide his revulsion. We are asked to admire Chingachgook, but also to wonder whether he is not acting in needlessly brutal ways. Leatherstocking's acceptance of scalping as an Indian custom does not preclude his racist wish that the victim had been a Mingo rather than a Frenchman. But another and even more important kind of double standard remains unresolved in this passage. Does Cooper hope that his reader, along with Hawkeye, will momentarily forget that colonial and provincial governments are in fact paying for the scalps harvested by their Indian mercenaries? If so, the reader would ascribe the barbarity of scalping solely to the Indian, enabling Cooper as narrator tacitly to condone the supposedly greater humanity of the white race.

When Cora first sees the "Indian runner" Magua, she looks at him with "an indescribable look of pity, admiration and horror" (24). Although the reader is given no reason why Magua should provoke so intense a response, Cooper clearly intends, at the book's outset, to indicate the complexity of responses we should maintain toward him. Pity and fear are the emotions Aristotle claimed were created and purged in a dramatic tragedy. Admiration or awe is the emotion that the hero of an epic poem evokes within its listeners or its readers. Because we rarely admire and fear those whom we also pity, only a convincingly deep character can evoke all three emotions. Our pity is extended to a tragic or epic hero, not because he is victimized, but because his great merits are destroyed by forces within as well as beyond him.

Cooper's word *horror* has, of course, connotations different from Aristotle's word *fear*. We fear the disintegration of people who have powerful virtues, but we feel horror when those virtues express themselves in perverse forms. Magua's atrocities, on which the plot's immediate impact depends, are kept plainly in evidence. Magua leads innocent people into ambush, abducts women, and threatens them with torture and concubinage. It is his "fatal and appalling whoop" (199) that signals the onset of the worst atrocity in the book, the planned massacre of an army that has already surrendered. As his single combat with Chingachgook shows, Magua is capable of great courage as well as cunning on the battlefield, but at the book's narrative climax, we see him as a crazed coward. After one of his Huron warriors knifes Cora, Magua vents his frustration first by stabbing Uncas, who is lying face down on the ground, then by "uttering an unearthly shout, as he committed the dastardly deed," and last by stabbing the helpless Uncas three times "with a look of inextinguishable scorn" (380).

Magua thus commits every act by which the cultural image of the bad Indian or evil savage was then defined. To turn *The Last of the Mohicans* into a vehicle for racial hatred has proved regrettably easy. All one needs to do is to forget, as Cooper's book never allows us to do, why Magua acts as he does. Before Magua tells Cora that her father had ordered him publicly whipped, Magua reveals that he had been a 20-year-old Huron chief before he saw a white man or tasted liquor. When Magua scornfully accuses his "Canada fathers" with the rhetorical questions "Who gave him the fire-water? who made him a villain," Cora tries to refute him by asking, "And am I answerable that thoughtless and unprincipled men exist, whose shades of countenance may resemble mine?" (117). In reply, Magua forces Cora to recognize that, although she bears no personal responsibility for Magua's degradation, her father's race does. He compels Cora to acknowledge that her father's presence at Fort William Henry is part of a military strategy involving the invasion of red lands: "The pale-faces have driven the red-skins from their hunting grounds, and now, when they fight, a white man leads the way" (117). Cora tries to avoid this larger charge by forcing it back to entirely personal grounds: "He [my father] forgot not his words, and did justice, by punishing the offender" (117). But Magua will not permit her narrow view to prevail. "Justice?" he says angrily; "is it justice to make evil, and then punish for it!" (117). Cooper's exclamation point shows that Magua's words are intended less as a rhetorical question than as a statement of fact. Magua's angry exposure of the injustice of white "justice" rightfully ends the exchange, reducing Cora to silence because "she knew not how to palliate this imprudent severity on the part of her father, in a manner to suit the comprehension of an Indian" (118). If, however, there is a defensible reply that might suit the comprehension of a white man, Cooper does not try to offer it. Magua's accounting, which transcends even pity, is allowed to prevail; his rage here serves as the voice of reason.

When the Delaware assemble in council to decide the fates of Uncas and Cora, Magua is permitted to speak in defense of his just right to retain his prisoner. Before he does so, he delivers the longest and surely the most forceful speech in the entire novel. Drawing on all the poetic power Cooper associated with Indian natural metaphor, Magua develops a view of Western settlement in which race, rather than politics, religion, or economics, is history's prevailing force. It is red men, Magua says, who were made in the image of the Great Spirit, red men to whom "He gave this island as he had made it," and red men who, in the old times, were "brave," " just," and "happy" (340). Although Magua ascribes Judeo-Christian ideas of Creation and Paradise to Indian mythology, thereby claiming primacy for his own race, he denigrates and quickly dismisses black people as sluggish bears, mere "slaves" ordered by the Great Spirit "to work for ever" (339). Peoples of color, in Magua's opinion, are evidently created unequal—a view suggesting Cooper's awareness that, in 1825, many a Cherokee was a slaveowner.

The rhetorical center of Magua's speech, however, is his attack on the white man:

"Some [men] he made with faces paler than the ermine of the forests; and these he ordered to be traders, dogs to their women, and wolves to their slaves. He gave this people the nature of the pigeon; wings that never tire; young, more plentiful than the leaves on the trees, and appetites to devour the earth. He gave them tongues like the false call of the wild-cat; hearts like rabbits; the cunning of the hog, (but none of the fox,) and arms longer than the legs of the moose. With his tongue, he stops the ears of the Indians; his heart teaches him to pay warriors to fight his battles; his cunning tells him how to get together the goods of the earth; and his arms enclose the land from the shores of the salt water, to the islands of the great lake. His gluttony makes him sick. God gave him enough, and yet he wants all. Such are the pale-faces." (339–40)

Except for the remark about white men being "dogs to their women," every phrase of Magua's speech seems an overstated but essentially accurate prophecy of the historical consequences of the white man's appetite for land. Magua is, of course, primarily concerned with the effect of the white man's appetite on Indians (dispossessed of their tribal lands), but he also considers the effects of the white man's invasion on blacks (worked by wolfish owners), on the land (devoured by imagined hunger), and ultimately on whites themselves (sick through their own gluttony). The white man's need to consume seems likely to destroy everything while truly absorbing nothing. Environmentalists and military historians, as well as Indians and Afro-Americans, must find prophetic truth in Magua's words. No impartial white reader, in Cooper's time or ours, can read them without at least a wince of shame.

Nonetheless, the fictional context of Magua's accusation lessens the authority of his words. Speaking before an Indian council, Magua is eager to appear as a red patriot and a persuasive orator so that he can strengthen his captor's claim to take Cora away. Magua's own appetite for vengeance is every bit as strong as the gluttony he ascribes to whites. And yet what Magua says at this moment will ultimately prove true to the world of the novel. Chingachgook and the narrator confirm Magua's insistence on Indian land possession by right of first occupancy; like him, they evoke a precolonial era of Indian contentment. British and French officers who talk of military honor while cutting bloody inroads into the forest make Magua's charge about white cunning seem plausible. The aged Tamenund, a voice of reasoned wisdom, will in fact echo Magua by saying, "I know that the pale-faces are a proud and hungry race" (344). When the Delaware (effectively neutral, officially allied to the British) and the Hurons (officially neutral, in fact allied to the French) fight each other in the second to last chapter, both tribes are unknowingly illustrating Magua's belief that intraracial genocide is proceeding through white treachery: "With his tongue, he stops the ear of the Indians; his heart teaches him to pay warriors to fight his battles" (340).

Magua vents racial accusations that Cooper hopes may prove exaggerated but that Cooper knows will be offensive to the contemporary white reader. Through the mouth of the novel's ostensible villain, Cooper can thus express damning truths without directly affirming them. Before condemning Cooper for the expediency of such a compromise, we should consider that convincing and memorable literary "villains" usually serve their author in exactly this way. The immediate case in point is John Milton's Satan, who, in his pride, eloquence, and drive for revenge, is Magua's prototype in previous epic literature. (At one point, Cooper remarks "it would not have been difficult to have fancied the dusky savage the Prince of Darkness, brooding on his own fancied wrongs, and plotting evil" [321]). If Milton was, as William Blake claimed, of the Devil's party without knowing it, we may also say that Cooper knowingly gave a red Satan just cause for revenge and then shuddered at the consequences.

Like every novel so influential that it has created as well as reaffirmed stereotypes, *The Last of the Mohicans* asks us to believe in characters who in a later era seem embarrassingly artificial. Recovering the original characters from half-forgotten memories of pulp-novel and B-movie versions becomes all the more essential. Uncas is not simply a noble Apollo, nor Chingachgook a stoic chieftain, nor Magua a red Devil. To restore them to the original complexity created by Cooper's words is to begin to appreciate the issues that first lent their characterization great cultural power.

The authority of Cooper's Indian characterizations must not be confused with authentic documentation of the way of life of the

Delaware, Iroquois, or any Eastern Woodland tribe of the eighteenth century. During Cooper's lifetime, almost all white writers who had lived among Indians were, as Cooper knew, Christian missionaries rather than trained observers of comparative customs. Not until the late nineteenth century did ethnologists (an early term for "anthropologists") begin visiting reservations and tribal communities. Cooper's personal experience of Indians remained limited to occasionally observing chieftains' state visits to Washington and Iroquois fringe communities in central New York. Consequently, he was in no position to pretend to sociological accuracy, nor did he wish to.

In the second volume of *The Last of the Mohicans*, the escape-pursuit sequences are twice halted to show us a Huron and then a Delaware council. But the perspective from which we enter and see these councils is the viewpoint of the white outsider whose purpose for being there is to reclaim a white captive. Factual detail can be kept minimal because the controlling concerns of these chapters are policy and power, not interracial cultural discovery. At the male-dominated Iroquois council, we overhear debates about defying the white man, and we see rites of torture that are far less sensational than those depicted in many a captivity narrative. At the Delaware council, we overhear policy speeches, but we also witness contests of skill and rites of hospitality in which women have an important function. These two councils provide contrasted models of Indian ceremonial life that somewhat conveniently take place, not amid the daily life of settled communities but during the temporary encampments of wartime. Although a few presumably factual details are adapted from Heckewelder (the name Tamenund, the turtle clan, the Delaware belief in the Manitto, etc.), the two elaborated council scenes give us a glimpse of a warrior-hunter culture whose customs recall those of Homeric Greeks. Appropriate chapter epigraphs from the *Iliad* suggest that Cooper wishes his prose fiction to be read in the context of Homer's epic poem, not as a missionary's account nor a Bureau of Indian Affairs policy paper.

Because Hawkeye's cultural relativism is well in advance of Cooper's time, it must have both an ambiguous source and an uncertain outcome. If, as Leatherstocking constantly says, it is an Indian's

"gift" to retaliate, to ambush his enemy, and to bear pain unflinchingly, is this gift an innate racial (i.e., "red") characteristic, or is it learned
behavior common to all hunter-warrior societies that still live in a
State of Nature? If the former, red and white are forever different—
perhaps ultimately one in God's eyes, but clearly separate on earth. If
the latter, red and white are in essence one humanity, whose observed
differences of behavior, beneath physiognomy and skin color, are
entirely attributable to social conditioning.

Cooper does not, fortunately, play God with his novel by pre-
suming to know the answer to this insoluble question. More often than
not, however, his sympathies seem to lie with a hopeful belief both in
universal humanity and in the primacy of environmental conditioning.
Leatherstocking's ringing affirmations of red monotheism, of the
Indian's love of family, and of the Indian's perception of God in
nature, all presume that the assumption of an ineradicable racial difference is "a wicked fabrication of the whites" (256). Conversely,
when Magua logically extends his belief in God-ordained racial differences into a call for a race war, he clearly speaks the Devil's suicidal
despair, even though a race war seems presently justified by white
colonial policies of divide and conquer.

Cooper wrote his summary statement on the vexed issue of
Indian character for the 1831 preface, five years after the novel was
published:

> Few men exhibit greater diversity, or, if we may so express it,
> greater antithesis of character, than the native warrior of North
> America. In war, he is daring, boastful, cunning, ruthless, self-
> denying, and self-devoted; in peace, just, generous, hospitable,
> revengeful, superstitious, modest, and commonly chaste. These
> are qualities, it is true, which do not distinguish all alike; but they
> are so far the predominating traits of these remarkable people, as
> to be characteristic. (7).

From the outset, the statement cites universal human terms of value
("Few men exhibit greater diversity . . . of character") rather than par-
ticularizing alternatives (e.g., "The Indian race exhibits great diversity

of indigenous traits"). The essence of the Indian, Cooper asserts, is not any set of special defining qualities but the very principle of "antithesis." The red man, he insists, is somehow both "self-denying" and "self-devoted" in war, both "generous" and "revengeful" in peace. Anyone who has read *The Last of the Mohicans* closely can recall instances in which Cooper's Indians plausibly exhibit all four of these antithetical qualities. The problem here, of course, is that Cooper's white characters also exhibit both sets of the same antithetical inner qualities, but the white person's generosity, revenge, self-denial, and self-devotion are expressed differently because they are shaped by different cultural practices. The question thus remains: In what essential trait do Indian character and white character truly differ? Setting out to establish a racial difference, Cooper's passage (perhaps unintentionally) has ended by implying that all human beings, regardless of race, are driven by similar kinds of antitheses.

Two of the book's emotional climaxes affirm the same kind of universalist assumptions. As the narrative ends, it becomes clear that no one has suffered more from Indian vengeance than Colonel Munro, whose soldiers have been treacherously butchered after their surrender, and whose eldest daughter has been twice abducted, threatened with rape, and then murdered. When it is Munro's turn to speak publicly to the assembled Delawares over the body of his daughter ("perhaps the greatest effort of which human nature is capable"), Munro suddenly and entirely relinquishes his military self: "Say to these kind and gentle females, that a heart-broken and failing man, returns them his thanks. Tell them, that the Being we all worship, under different names, will be mindful of their charity; and that the time shall not be distant, when we may assemble around his throne, without distinction of sex, or rank, or colour!" (391). Leatherstocking shakes his head at Munro's surprising acceptance of the Indian's humanity, not because Hawkeye is sure Munro is wrong (Hawkeye says the same thing on occasion) but because most other whites will never be brought to share Munro's feelings.

Quite clearly, the pressure of extreme grief has brought Munro to recognize that interracial oneness must transcend earthly time.

Similarly, when Hawkeye and Chingachgook stand over the body of Uncas, they are joined in a way that knows no race: "Chingachgook grasped the hand that, in the warmth of feeling, the scout had stretched across the fresh earth, and in that attitude of friendship, these two sturdy and intrepid woodmen bowed their heads together, while scalding tears fell to their feet, watering the grave of Uncas, like drops of falling rain" (394). At the moment when Uncas's natural father and his adopted father join hands in mourning for their lost son, their identities as the Big Serpent and as Natty Bumppo are lost in the commonality of their being "these two sturdy and intrepid woodmen." It is a moment of a human feeling that transcends separate human identites, when red and white show their manliness through the intensity of their weeping. But like Munro's forgiveness, it is a moment only, a glimpse of an aracial world that lies within present human capacity only at times of severest loss.

GENDER

Throughout nineteenth-century America, gender roles remained widely separate despite mounting protest. In James Fenimore Cooper's time, a married woman (legally, a *femme coverte*) could not own property, could not sue in court, and could not retain her children in the unlikely event of divorce. Virtually deprived of legal existence, women could neither vote nor join most public organizations. Except for schoolteaching and, somewhat later, nursing and mill labor, women could not be publicly employed. They were expected to marry, to bear children, and to serve as the mainstay of the family; an unmarried woman was likely to spend her days living as a "spinster" aunt in a sibling's home. Woman's world was rigidly domestic, her separate sphere guardedly private.

Public powerlessness did not mean, however, that her role in society was considered unimportant. Until industrialization gathered force in the 1840s, most women fulfilled essential roles within the complex economies of self-sufficient farms and artisan households. Throughout the century, a young woman would continue to be expected to become wife and mother, domestic helpmeet and family nurse, the guardian both of Christian religion and of her children's upbringing. For these purposes, middle- and upper-class women were educated to acquire foreign languages and knowledge of the fine arts, including literature. Such a genteel education made single women increasingly desirable in marriage. As wives became consumers rather than producers, their refinement became a badge of family culture. Well before midcentury, it was commonly believed that a mother's moral and aesthetic sensitivity showed the propriety of insulating the family from the mire of male public life.

Such extreme and growing separation of gender roles made it difficult for male writers to see in their women characters anything beyond projections of their own desires and fears. The concerns of the historical novel—so public, political, and military—would seem to be wholly removed from women's restricted world. What connection could there be between the books on the sofa table in a middle-class woman's parlor in 1826 and the army-ridden forests beyond Lake George in 1757? It is not surprising that, at the end of his first preface to *The Last of the Mohicans*, Cooper sounds conspicuously edgy about his readers:

> With this brief introduction to his subject, then, the author com-
> mits his book to the reader. As, however, candour, if not justice,
> requires such a declaration at his hands, he will advise all young
> ladies, whose ideas are usually limited by the four walls of a com-
> fortable drawing room; all single gentlemen, of a certain age, who
> are under the influence of the winds; and all clergymen, if they
> have the volumes in hand, with intent to read them, to abandon
> the design. He gives this advice to such young ladies, because,
> after they have read the book, they will surely pronounce it
> shocking; to the bachelors, as it might disturb their sleep; and to
> the reverend clergy, because they might be better employed. (6)

Three kinds of unlikely readers are here confronted with the lure of the abominable, thus turning Cooper's seeming prohibition into an invitation. The novel's killings, Cooper well knows, are so bloody and sadistic that every reader, not just a young lady, must find them shock-

ing. Even Colonel Munro—an able and experienced military commander—becomes so shattered by frontier brutality and military treachery
that he abandons all pretense of male leadership. In one sense, Cooper
was the very bachelor he postulates: Cooper wrote much of the book,
probably including the especially nightmarish section of chapters 5–13,
in New York City during a time of sleeplessness, intermittent fever,
and separation from his wife. The clerical reader "might be better
employed" on his pastoral tasks only if he wishes to ignore truths
understandable through fiction but not through Scripture. Instead of
singling out these three groups of readers in order to shut them out, as
he claims to do, Cooper is inviting them in by challenging them with
"shocking" subjects yet to be disclosed. The ensuing narrative will test
rather than exclude them. Into the midst of a world of male frontier
warfare, so purportedly alien to bachelors, clergyman, and young
ladies, Cooper places two bachelors, a psalmodist, and two unmarried
young women.

In characterizing women, male writers of nineteenth-century
romantic fiction returned almost obsessively to imagining variant versions of two simplistic archetypes known as the Fair Lady and the
Dark Lady. The Fair Lady—blond-haired, blue-eyed, and fully
Caucasian—represents both the value of civil society and a curious
innocence about it. Her responses are passive and her ideas conven-
tional; she is physically weak, deferential to males, easily shocked, but
innately decent. The Dark Lady—dark-haired, dark-eyed, and often
"tainted" by Jewish or black blood—represents the attractions of social
rebellion and forbidden knowledge. In Scott's novels, the Dark Lady
(Flora MacIvor, Rebecca) is likely to be a high-minded loyalist or
utopian committed to lost rebellions, whereas the Fair Lady (Rose,
Rowena) quietly awaits her prosperous domestic future in the new
order. The hero wavers between them, as he does between the political causes they embody. He may be emotionally and intellectually
attracted to the Dark Lady, but at novel's end, he readily reconciles
himself to marrying the Fair Lady.

These paired heroines may be found everywhere in the major
writings of canonical male writers of nineteenth-century American fiction: Poe's Ligeia and Rowena ("Ligeia"), Hawthorne's Zenobia and

Priscilla (*The Blithedale Romance*), Melville's Isabel and Lucy (*Pierre*), followed by Realist reformulations in Howells's Penelope and Irene (*The Rise of Silas Lapham*) and James's Olive and Verena (*The Bostonians*). In imaginative origin, the paired ladies are as fully symbiotic as the "good" and "bad" Indian. In all but three of the fictions listed, the Fair Lady and the Dark Lady are revealed to be sisters, the offspring often of one father but of different mothers. Their ultimate father, however, is the novelist himself, who gives life to his heroines out of imagined contrary needs: mistress versus wife, soulmate versus helpmeet, freedom versus respectability, and aesthetics versus assets. The wavering between these two views of woman is thus transferred from the novelist to his protagonist. As fictional renditions of the paired heroines accumulate through the century, a crucial problem of resolution becomes increasingly apparent. Might the final sacrifice of the Dark Lady to the demands of social progress be, not a happy ending, but a surrender of the self's true and long-denied vitality?

In American romantic fiction, the prototypes of the paired Fair and Dark sisters are Alice and Cora Munro: Alice (Latin "light"), of all-white blood, whose golden hair, blue eyes, green veil, and insistently genteel speech mark her as young, innocent, and infinitely marriageable to the handsome colonial officer, and Cora (Latin "heart"), of part-black blood, whose black hair, black eyes, and frank words mark her as older, far more knowing, and possibly marriageable to the last of the Mohicans, but not to the white officer destined for prominence in a settled community. What functions do they serve in this particular narrative? Why indeed are they here at all?

The historian's response—that there had been wives, daughters, and women servants among the British troops at Fort William Henry in 1757—is not a plausible answer. Cooper wished his rendering of the massacre to be accurate, but he never felt obliged to include historical persons simply because they had been there. Nor does Cooper feel compelled to set Alice and Cora down amid the French and Indian War simply because Rose and Flora had been in the Jacobite Rebellion, or Rowena and Rebecca in the Anglo-Norman wars: Cooper would often ignore Scott's precedent when it suited him. The protagonists of captivity narratives were not always women (i.e.,

John Williams). Had Cooper wished to secure the readership of novels by Suzannah Rowson and Hannah Foster, he could have devised a new variation on the seduction plot. There were recent models of very different fictional women under duress on civilization's borders (including Ann Eliza Bleecker's Maria Kittle and Cooper's own Betty Flanagan) whose presence would perhaps have been more plausible. Why, then, does Cooper wish to make us feel the constant presence of young women like Cora and Alice on the far reaches of the frontier?

A partial answer can be suggested by linking Cora and Alice to the legendary historical figure of Jane McCrae, who, like Cora and Alice, had left Fort Edward under the protection of Indian escorts supposedly allied to the British Army. When the body of Jane McCrae was found scalped in the forest, her fate became an important source of Revolutionary War propaganda against the British and their Indian allies. Like John Vanderlyn's painting *Death of Jane McCrea* (1804), which Cooper almost surely saw exhibited in New York City in 1825, *The Last of the Mohicans* focuses, on five separate occasions, on vengeful, overpowering savages who are about to kill and scalp a white maiden dressed in functionally inappropriate but sexually arousing clothing. In Cooper's prose as in Vanderlyn's painting, the impending horror of scalping is frozen at exactly the moment when Nature's Roman dissolves into the brute: "Seizing Cora by the rich tresses which fell in confusion about her form, he [a nameless Huron] tore her from her frantic hold, and bowed her down with brutal violence to her knees. The savage drew the flowing curls through his hand, and raising them on high with an outstretched arm, he passed the knife around the exquisitely moulded head of his victim, with a taunting and exulting laugh" (129).

Although this particular image of sexual violence is repeatedly used to horrify and arouse the reader, Cooper never allows the threatening moment to be consummated. Thanks to timely rescues, Alice survives all attacks of this kind. Magua may look at Cora with "an expression no chaste female might endure" (119), but Cora proves far too courageous to be violated. Readers often forget that Cora is murdered not by the lustful Magua but by one of Magua's Hurons, who is

John Vanderlyn, *The Death of Jane McCrea*, 1804. Wadsworth Atheneum, Hartford.

driven by perverse loyalty. In plotting his novel, Cooper does all he can to underscore the power of courageous people in incidental, temporary crises. Because he has such difficulty justifying the spread of civilization in broad historical terms, Cooper thus turns his plot in ways that justify the westward march of empire through character association. By transporting fair and dark ladies through the wilderness to Fort William Henry, four courageous fictional men (two red and two white) can show that they are, as Duncan Heyward says, in a situation where "a man would be ashamed to prove other than a hero" (95). Before the Hurons attack the cave at Glenn's Falls, Hawkeye defines his mission as the preserving of "these tender blossoms from the fangs of the worst of serpents" (54). "These Mohicans and I," he says, repeating the metaphor, "will do what man's thoughts can invent to keep such flowers, which, though so sweet, were never made for the wilderness, from harm" (46). As such statements accumulate, the Fair and Dark maidens increasingly seem to represent icons of a feminine civilization. To carry them unmolested and unharmed through the wilderness becomes an implied justification of not only individual male prowess but the spread of civilization itself. Although Cooper cannot honestly justify white conquest in his fiction's history, he passingly reassures readers by placing archetypal characters in the contrived situations of history's fictions.

Twentieth-century readers should beware of assuming that Alice Munro's helplessness was not as absurd to Cooper as it is to us. Her first sight of Magua brings forth her first words: "Are such spectres frequent in the woods, Heyward; or is this sight an especial entertainment, ordered on our behalf? If the latter, gratitude must close our mouths; but if the former, both Cora and I shall have need to draw largely on that stock of hereditary courage of which we boast, even before we are made to encounter the redoubtable Montcalm" (25). These are the overelaborate words of someone who knows she has no knowledge of the forest, no survival skills whatever, yet who tries to pretend, through the formality of her speech, that she is safely witnessing an "especial entertainment" for someone of her genteel culture to appreciate. Alice's premonition that she will need courage proves correct, but she tries to speak with a levity that will somehow keep her above her situation. Cooper, however, does not allow Alice's bravado to rest unchallenged. When Heyward replies that Magua will be leading them through the forest and off the troop road, Alice's parade of self-control promptly collapses into "real terror" as she shudders out the simple words "I like him not" (25).

Again and again, Cooper will repeat this same pattern: Alice's pretense of ladylike control, the exposure of Alice's ignorance, her relapse into immobile terror, and her need for male rescue. Helpless in all practical matters, Alice is undone by physically threatening situations. Her one admirable moment comes when she declares that, rather than be freed in exchange for Cora's agreeing to submit to Magua, she would rather die by torture. It is, fittingly, a moment of clear moral decision in which physical courage needs only to be anticipated. For the most part, however, Alice remains a weepy encumbrance whose helplessness, however much it may elicit male heroism, does little to show the preferability of the Fair Lady. Duncan Heyward's love for Alice is based in part on his possessing the same high-minded and innocent ineptitude. Their future marital bliss is disposed of in one sentence. When Cooper tells us that the couple are departing "far into the settlements of the 'pale-faces'" (392), the novel's "happy ending" looks suspiciously like a retreat.

Cora has exactly those inner strengths which Alice conspicuously lacks. Physically as well as morally courageous, Cora understands the tactics of forest survival as soon as they are explained to her—and then practices them. When surrounded by Hurons at Glenn's Falls, Alice sinks to the cave's floor, sobbing out barren emotional regret for having been selfish in insisting on seeking out her father. Cora calmly replies that she intends at the least to prove to her father "that however others might neglect him, in his strait, his children at least were faithful" (71). Whereas Alice speaks the overblown language of sentiment, Cora's words are clear, controlled, dignified. Perhaps because she is conscious of her black blood, Cora feels no need to pretend to a gentility she cannot have. Magua lusts after Cora and Uncas lovingly admires her; Uncas pities Alice and Magua has contempt for her. To all characters who understand the forest, Cora seems a significant human being but Alice remains at best a "tender blossom."

Because Cora is so clearly admirable, her responses to her own sexuality and to her mixed blood prove as troublesome to Cooper as to us. As one might expect of anyone in Cooper's day who passed for white, Cora is secretly ashamed of her black blood. When she acknowledges to Tamenund that "the curse of my ancestors has fallen heavily on their child," she speaks with embarrassed shame, "suffering her head to droop, until her burning cheeks were nearly concealed in the maze of dark, glossy tresses" (344). And yet, as we have seen, Cora's blackness has in other ways been repeatedly connected to both her competence and her courage. Her shame at being part Negro in no way lessens her outrage at Magua's sexual advances toward her. Her revulsion for him is primarily caused by abduction and threatened rape, but it is also revulsion at becoming the concubine of a red man. While Cora watches Magua preparing to torture Alice as his way of forcing Cora to relent, Cora first denounces Magua as "a savage, a barbarous and ignorant savage" and then publicly dismisses him by crying out, "Leave me . . . you mingle bitterness in my prayers; you stand between me and my God!" (124). Cora's admirable courage is here expressed in blatantly racist terms. As we approve of her courage, are we also asked to accept her notion of red savagery, or to believe that there is one God for white and black people but another for red?

In such moments, Cora becomes an outlet for racist responses aroused by Cooper's plot. Cora is also, however, a fully sexual woman who can fulfill male codes of heroic conduct, yet has as much "heart" as anyone of either gender. Possessing black blood in addition to all these complexities, Cora is one of those characters who show us both the limitations of society's racial and gender boundaries and the dangers of stepping over them. Just as Hawkeye is a "man without a cross," so Cora is a "woman with a cross." If her mixed blood were fully known, she could occupy no place in "civilized" society worthy of her abilities. Were she willing to share Uncas's life, she would either have to seek out a vanishing Delaware community or complicate the interracial male bonds of those men she most admires. Cooper must kill her off, sacrifice her to the continuation of two kinds of societies. But he does so with one of the most astonishing tributes the Dark Lady of nineteenth-century fictional romance would ever receive. Longstanding associations of black with evil are challenged. At the moment when Cora is murdered, she is wearing a white robe. As the Delaware maidens mourn over Cora's body, singing of her beauty and her courage, of her reunion with Uncas in the afterlife, they insist "that she was of a *blood purer and richer* than the rest of her nation" (386, italics mine). Hawkeye may shake his head in disapproval at these words, but Cooper as narrator provides no response to them. The Delaware maidens' song, we may conclude, is certainly not to be regarded as simply "wrong"; rather, it calls for an alternate vision of race and gender, a realigning of what it might mean to be male and female, red and black and white. In 1757, in 1826, or in the 1990s, the maidens' song envisions a time that, if it ever existed, is both clearly past and not yet come again.

The frontier of 1757, red and white, is not only controlled by men; it is nominally dominated by patriarchs whose authority depends on their rank, wisdom, military prowess, and honorable loyalty to tribe or nation. Despite her many-sided rebelliousness, Cora defers to the power of patriarchy when it is honorably exercised. The loving, dutiful daughter of a white patriarch, Cora kneels before the ultimate red patriarch, Tamenund (see Cole's painting on the cover) in order to plead for Alice's freedom and against bloodshed. To Cora, Tamenund is "the father—the judge—I had almost said the prophet—of this people" (343), a gathering of roles that suggests the Deity. It is therefore not surprising that at the climactic moment of pursuit, Cora is willing to kneel before the patriarch of Heaven and Earth. When Hawkeye and Uncas finally catch up with Magua (atop a precipice, of course), Magua draws his knife, turns to Cora, and declares, "Woman, choose; the wigwam or the knife of le Subtil!" (379):

> Cora regarded him not; but dropping on her knees, she raised her eyes and stretched her arms towards Heaven, saying, in a meek and yet confiding voice—
> "I am thine! do with me as thou seest best!" (379)

Magua, as Cora knows, has reclaimed due patriarchal authority among the Hurons by dishonorable means. As she kneels, first before

Tamenund and now before God, Cora knows she has no choice but to appeal to the true patriarch as the only means of freeing herself from the false one.

In both instances, the patriarchs conspicuously fail her. Tamenund, committed to a warrior's right to his war prisoner as a matter of tribal honor, relinquishes Cora to Magua, thus precipitating Cora's death and intertribal killing between Hurons and Delawares. Then, a scant two paragraphs after Cora has pleaded to God, "I am thine! do with me as thou seest best!," she is murdered by a follower of Magua, who, "profiting by the chance, sheathed his own knife" in her bosom (379). Unless we are to assume that Tamenund has finally become senile, we must conclude that a warrior's code of honor will inevitably lead to cruel and unnecessary tribal killing. Similarly, unless we assume that God is sadistic, or Cora's death just, we must conclude that the Deity, if He exists, seems somehow not even to have heard Cora's words.

The Last of the Mohicans certainly does not empower women, but it does disempower men. Duncan Heyward's ineptitude is so transparent that Hawkeye at one point contemptuously tells him that the best service he can perform is to "keep in our rear, and be careful not to cross the trail" (213). Because of his cowardice, Reed-That-Bends is stripped of his name, his tribal identity, and all sense of self. Uncas and Magua are killed. Every red chieftain dies without issue. No mention is made of any children born to the marriage of Alice Munro and Duncan Heyward. Hawkeye and Chingachgook survive with all their individual powers intact but with no community to serve. The single most dramatic disempowering of male authority is inflicted on Colonel Munro, who is not only honest and honorable but the white English-speaking male of highest station whom we see in the novel. Cooper's concluding scene asks us to listen, again and again, to the mourning words of barren patriarchs (Munro, Chingachgook, Hawkeye, and Tamenund), each of whom laments the loss of a blood child or of his adopted children. The conquering of the American frontier, the warfare between nations and races, demands male heroism and then disillusions or destroys those who exhibit it. Patriarchs are allowed to have the last word, but they speak not of rebuilding but of the power vacuum left behind by bloodshed.

Cooper's contemporaries liked to argue that the male Indian's abusive treatment of his women was proof of civilization's superiority to savagery. Ignoring the divisions of labor, as well as the matrilineal and matrilocal customs of many tribes, white authors wrote of Indian women as degraded "slaves" who tended the fields and served the sexual needs of proud warriors. Even Thomas Jefferson, it was often noted, had been forced to acknowledge, while defending the humanity of the Indian, that "the women are submitted to unjust drudgery. This I believe is the case with every barbarous people. . . . It is civilization alone which replaces women in the enjoyment of their natural equality."[8] Whatever be the ironies of the claim that only civilization can restore women to "natural equality," *The Last of the Mohicans* certainly does not reinforce—indeed, it subverts—consoling contemporary clichés about Indian women. Magua would like to treat Cora as both a drudge and a concubine, it is true, but his desire to do so persistently villainizes him. More important, Cooper never claims that Magua's desire for a servant-wife is at all characteristic of Magua's race.

Instead, as in later Leatherstocking Tales, Cooper divides his brief characterizations of Indian women into two kinds: (a) young Indian women of marriageable age and fine feelings, whose firm tribal loyalty does not conflict with their love for warriors as individuals, and (b) old Indian crones, no longer fit for the field or the marriage bed, who exult in the torture of captives, especially if the captive is young, red, and desirable. The Delaware maidens are women of the first kind; the Huron "squaw" who tortures Uncas is of the second:

> The crafty squaw, who had taken the necessary precaution to fire the piles, made her way through the throng, and cleared a place for herself in front of the captive. The squalid and withered person of this hag, might well have obtained for her the character of possessing more than human cunning. Throwing back her light vestment, she stretched forth her long skinny arm in derision. . . . 'Look you, Delaware!, . . . your nation is a race of women, and the hoe is better fitted to your hands than the gun! (272).

Older Puritan imaginings of the witch seem here to have been transformed into newer forms of female deviltry. The old Indian woman's delight in torture seems a sadistic displacement for her now useless sexuality. The hag and the maiden, who would resurface in both Simms's *The Yemassee* (1835) and Longfellow's *Hiawatha* (1855), supplanted the notion of the drudge only to become clichés themselves. These symbiotic characterizations, rather than showing the red person to be inferior to the white, implied that women of both races derive their identity from their marital relations to men. The ultimate insult the Huron crone hurls at Uncas is that his tribe is a race of women and that he is assuming an outmoded women's role.

Feminist scholars interested in gender criticism have recently focused attention on two long-dismissed novels about white-red historical conflicts written by women contemporaries of Cooper: Lydia Maria Child's *Hobomok* (1824) and Catharine Maria Sedgwick's *Hope Leslie* (1827). Whenever scholars presuppose that Cooper was simply the spokesman for contemporary racist and sexist attitudes, and never their critic, they do Cooper an injustice, setting up a straw man who is then promptly faulted for not anticipating today's multicultural or feminist perspectives. Whatever may be the literary merits of Child's and Sedgwick's novels (their narratives seem more incredible and disjointed than Cooper's, their dialogue even more stilted), comparing the three novels serves to clarify authorial gender roles. Cooper's focus is on interracial and intercolonial warfare, on ethical questions pertaining to physical survival in the wilderness. Child and Sedgwick quote male historical sources from time to time, but their main concerns (20 years before the rise of the "women's domestic novel") are insistently domestic and familial. For Child and Sedgwick, unlike Cooper, colonial history and barely tracked forests provide the framing settings rather than the subject of fiction; their interest is in the ways the love between man and woman, parent and child, either adapts to or breaks under the interpersonal tensions caused by racial and religious bigotry. The reader of *The Last of the Mohicans* places fictive incidents in the forest in the context of white and red battle codes, of intertribal and interracial conflict, of the struggle of French, British, and colonial powers for possession of a New World. For Child and Sedgwick, the three-sided feelings among Hobomok, Goodman Conant, and his daughter Mary, or among Magawisca, Hope Leslie, and Everell Fletcher, are the heart of the matter; historical concerns of race and empire are important when they impinge on and alter those feelings.

The main consequence of the difference is that, for both women authors, the issue of interracial love becomes the novel's center. Whereas Cooper repeatedly devises circumstances that prevent the mutual attraction between Uncas and Cora from leading to open passion, marriage, or children, Child and Sedgwick explore those very possibilities. After Charles Brown is exiled for heresy, Child's Mary Conant marries Hobomok, a Wampanoag friendly to the Puritans, and bears a son. Similarly, Hope Leslie's sister Faith marries the Pequod Oneco; at novel's end, Faith becomes fully acculturated to Indian ways. Up to a point, Hobomok can be seen as a prototype for Uncas: Nature's Roman, elevated beyond his people, who sustains relationships of great trust among whites without losing his Indian identity. Sedgwick, however, who refers to *The Last of the Mohicans* simply as "a recently published work," empowers red women to a degree perhaps unacceptable to Child and clearly unacceptable to Cooper.[9] Instead of brief appearances of Delaware maidens and Huron crones, Sedgwick endows her Pequod heroine Magawisca with the physical courage necessary first to save her adopted white mother from Indian murder, and then to save her beloved Everell (a kind of white foster brother) from Indian sacrifice. Magawisca denounces acts of red savagery and Puritan bigotry, of red vengeance and white imperialism. Remarkably like Leatherstocking entering Judge Temple's court in *The Pioneers* (1823), Magawisca stands defiantly in native garb before Governor Winthrop in order first to show and then to say that Winthrop's court has no jurisdiction over prior inhabitants of the land (286–87).

Just as it is currently easy to ignore Cooper's exposure of the weakness of all patriarchs, so it is equally easy to assume that a woman author's attack on patriarchy has little if any limit. In fact, however, Child seeks to convince us at the outset that Puritan forefathers were the "van-guard in the proud and rapid march of freedom," early civil libertarians who "kept the sacred flame still burning deeply and fervently."[10] Sedgwick concludes that New England's patriarchs were "noble pilgrims," "an exiled and suffering people" who "came forth in the dignity of the chosen servants of the Lord to open the forests to the sun-beam" and "to restore man—man oppressed and trampled on by his fellow; to religious and civil liberty, and equal rights" (Sedgwick, 72–73).

Child's and Sedgwick's fundamental allegiance to white domestic family values, rather than to Indian protest or to anything resembling multiculturalism, is apparent in the outcome of their interracial marriage plots. Shortly after the handsome and cavalierlike Charles Brown has returned alive from exile, Mary Conant marries him in a true Christian ceremony. Charles Hobomok Brown, her half-red son, will happily become "a distinguished graduate at Cambridge," losing all trace of his red identity (Child, 149–50). Once Hope Leslie and Everell Fletcher feel free of all scruples of guilt for having possibly trifled with Magawisca's feelings, they too are destined to marry and to assume a position in white society remarkably like that of Duncan Heyward and Alice Munro.

The happy endings in *Hobomok* and *Hope Leslie* ask the reader to admire the ethical enlightenment of an Indian who grandly and sadly sacrifices his or her (red) feelings for the sake of the future happiness of his or her (white) beloved. There is more than a whiff of racial condescension in arranging such convenient, high-minded renunciations and then celebrating them as natural or womanly feeling. Neither Chingachgook, Uncas, nor even Magua is ever forced to exemplify such an implausible (and ultimately degrading) racial "nobility."

6

History and Empire

Influential early modernists like E. M. Forster and Henry James attacked the historical novel as a forced hybrid, even a bastard, a literary form that has neither the accuracy of history nor the imaginative freedom of fiction. The very existence of a work like Tolstoy's *War and Peace,* as well as many superb historical novels of lesser note, including *The Last of the Mohicans,* discredits this charge. The opposing degrees of truth connoted by the very words *history* and *fiction* mislead us when those words refer to genres of writing. Neither the facts nor the patterns set forth by professional historians are always accurate and true. Nor is a novelist's imagined re-creation of a historical event necessarily inaccurate or fictional. At his best, the historical novelist reveals history to us, first by knowing the verifiable truth of the past thoroughly, and then by giving us an imagined re-creation of that past. The imagined past not only can possess accuracy, vividness, and narrative power (many histories have these merits) but it can have a special sharpness of focus that derives from the novelist's privilege of selectivity. However, the novelist's liberty to choose can also encourage distortion in re-creating the past—as in Cooper's account of racial difference and racial politics.

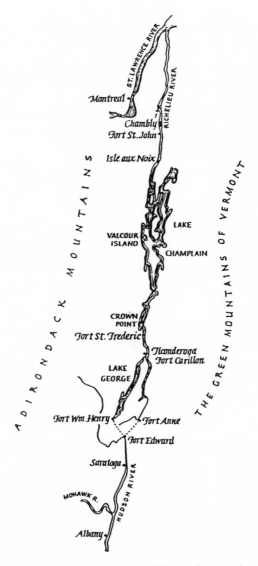

The water route from Montreal to Albany during the eighteenth century.

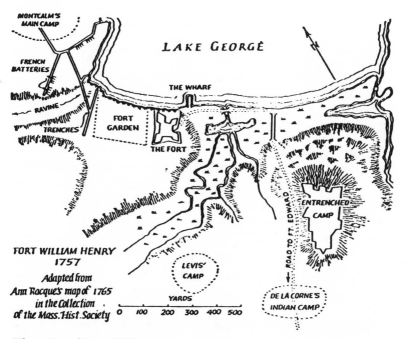

The seige of Fort Wiliam Henry, August 1757. Both maps are reproduced from Edward P. Hamilton's *The French and Indian Wars* (Doubleday & Co., 1962).

A very few historical novels, *The Last of the Mohicans* among them, have acted on history as well as revealed it. That is, a historical novel's portrayal of a past conflict, when that portrayal is powerful and widely known, can influence readers' attitudes toward present crises in which a similar conflict recurs. Such novels become a part of social as well as literary history; they are now increasingly becoming a part of the historian's history as well. For nineteenth-century readers, *The Last of the Mohicans* not only recovered the not so distant past of the French and Indian War; Cooper's rendering of red-white power relations shaped readers' responses both toward the Indian Removal controversy of the 1830s and toward a future continental empire that was to be American, rather than French or British.

Cooper began his first preface to *The Last of the Mohicans* with the forceful claim that the novel should be regarded as a historical "narrative" rather than an "imaginary and romantic picture of things which never had an existence" (3). At the exact center of Cooper's narrative is his rendering of the most notorious event of the French and Indian War, the so-called massacre of British troops, women, and children by General Montcalm's Indian allies after the British surrender of Fort William Henry to the French on 9 August 1757. Cooper's account of the surrender and the massacre (chapters 15–17) is, as we shall see, superb historical fiction: effectively paced, visually dramatic, yet true to known sources. Within the novel as a whole, however, the fall of Fort William Henry serves as a lens on the past, as a central historical exemplum around which a particular view of red-white and intercolonial conflicts can be developed. Because Cooper's first published words about his book claim essential accuracy for his entire narrative, we need to clarify the ways in which *The Last of the Mohicans* alters or confirms the past as we now know it. As Duncan Heyward and the Royal Americans set off to escort Colonel Munro's daughters to the fort, they enter into a world of treacherous historical complexity, much of which is as unknown to the reader as it is to them.

When the struggle between the French and the English for control of North America became acute in the late seventeenth century, the obstacle or buffer between the two imperial powers was the presence of the Five Nations of Iroquois, who controlled almost all of what is now New York State. From west to east, the tribes were the Seneca, Cayuga, Onondaga, Oneida, and Mohawk; these five were joined by the Tuscarora to form the Six Nations in 1711. Cooper is correct in portraying the Iroquois as ferocious warriors who practiced torture and who covered their skins with bear grease and red ocher— as much for protection against the weather as for war paint. But his historical need to picture groups of Indians as they gathered in the temporary military camps of 1757 leads Cooper to misrepresent the daily lives of northeastern Indian tribes. Neither the Iroquois, the Delaware, nor the Hurons were nomadic hunter-warriors who lived for the chase and for battle. As early as 1650, all five Iroqouis tribes were fundamentally agricultural, living in palisaded towns containing a longhouse and many family houses, matrilinearly grouped by clan. The Iroquois built barns, log houses, and stone fireplaces; they raised maize, beans, squash, and sunflowers; they cultivated and maintained orchards. Iroquois power clearly derived from their economy as well as from their league of peace. Because they were a settled, agricultural, and inland people, they were less dependent on British and French fur traders than the Algonquin tribes along the Atlantic seaboard. A hasty reader of Cooper's day who knew little about Indians beyond *The Last of the Mohicans*, however, could readily have assumed that, because the Mohawks or Hurons or Delawares did not seem to have cultivated the land, neither they nor any other eastern tribe had a right to possess the land, and could therefore be removed from it.

As English settlement pressed west and north from Albany after 1675, while French traders, priests, and soldiers pressed west and south from Montreal, it became increasingly difficult for the Iroquois to preserve both their independence from white nations and their league among themselves. The easternmost of the Five Nations, the Mohawk, were openly courted by the powerful English Superintendent of Indian Affairs, William Johnson, who welcomed them to his trading post and home near present-day Amsterdam, New York. Most of the northern tribe called the Hurons who, contrary to the impression of Cooper's novel, were not allied with the Iroquois League, became undeclared supporters of the French, as did the westernmost tribe, the Senecas. Tribes in the central part of the state, including the Oneida near the future site of Cooperstown, had less difficulty maintaining the league's official power of neutrality. The Mohawk, closest to the expanding settlements of colonists from New England and New York, were necessarily the most susceptible to the offers and threats of the British. For all Iroquois, however, the danger of white incursion on Iroquois lands and culture had to be balanced against the immediate benefits of acquiring the white man's goods, which included iron axes, iron ploughs, and iron guns, as much as the liquor or trinkets that Cooper emphasizes.

Cooper rightly wishes his reader to know, however, that all northeastern tribes were being caught between the closing blades of two imperial powers. British and French officials sometimes openly paid their Indian allies for the scalps as well as the prisoners of whites and reds on the other side. Hurons and Oneidas, ostensibly allied, were in fact fighting on different sides. Contingents within both the Delaware and the Mohawk were fighting against members of their own tribe. Hawkeye tells Uncas a historical fact that Uncas clearly knows but that the reader may not: "It is true, that white cunning has managed to throw the tribes into great confusion, as respects friends and enemies . . . thus throwing every thing into disorder, and destroying all the harmony of warfare" (223–24). A white policy of divide and conquer was clearly leading not just to thwarting the other European power but also to a self-destructive civil war between and within the Indian nations. Chingachgook is first described as a warrior on the warpath against Mingos, but we are immediately told that he carries "a tomahawk and scalping-knife, of English manufacture" (35). It is clearly the Europeans who are providing the Indians with the technological advances by which they can kill each other. Chingachgook's very first words in the novel are an unanswerable challenge to Cooper's white hero: "My fathers fought with the naked red-man! . . . Is there no difference, Hawk-eye, between the stone-headed arrow of the warrior, and the leaden bullet with which you kill?" (36).

The Mohegan (Cooper's "Mohican") Indians were an Algonquin tribe inhabiting coastal Connecticut near the Thames River. Soon after the arrival of the Puritans in the 1630s, Mohegan chief Uncas and his warriors fought with the whites against the Pequots in a war of dispossession and virtual genocide. Again in the 1670s, Uncas and the Mohegans joined white troops against the Wampanoags and their chief Metacomet (King Philip) in a war that virtually ended Indian power in New England. In nineteenth-century terminology, the historical Uncas was a "progressive" Indian (one who accepts acculturation and militarily sides with the white man) rather than a "Red Stick" Indian (one who fights the whites to preserve tribal culture and power). Were Cooper's Magua not allied with the French, he could be considered a Red Stick. Were Chingachgook and Uncas not trying to preserve Mohegan-Delaware ways of life, they could be considered progressive. Cooper complicates both stereotypes in order to suggest that the conflict is not so simple as a racial war or an inter-imperial war, but a perplexing cross between them.

The historical Uncas's "loyalty" to the English, however, did not preserve his own tribe. Driven westward toward Mohawk territory, some Mohegans were absorbed by the few Delaware then remaining in what is now northeastern Pennsylvania. During the American Revolution, other Mohegans joined remnants of the Mahicans (a separate upper–Hudson Valley tribe) living at Stockbridge, Massachusetts, where they were converted to Christianity by Moravian missionaries. Still others would settle in the tribally mixed Indian community at Brotherton, New York, south of Utica in Oneida County. Throughout the five-novel series, Leatherstocking is described as having been raised by Moravian missionaries who live in proximity to Delawares and Mohegans. During the 1760s, a remnant of the Mohegans at Stockbridge migrated to live among the Oneidas at New Stockbridge, New York, where Reverend Samuel Kirkland, who was to support the American Revolution, ran a mission. In the 1820s, Cooper probably saw descendants of these Christianized Mohegans living among the Oneida not far from Cooperstown.

After the Susquehanna tribe of the Delaware Indians were defeated by the Iroquois in the 1670s, the Delaware became an increasingly subservient nation; its members were regarded by the Iroquois as "women." Delaware chief Tamany had been a legendary figure of aged Indian wisdom before New York politicians founded Tammany Hall or James Fenimore Cooper created Tamenund. In Cooper's novel,

Tamenund mourns the folly of the loss of his tribal lands; one of the few facts known about Tamany, however, is that he had, at least twice during the 1690s, sold Delaware lands to William Penn. By the early 1700s, the Iroquois had become so dominant that they were selling former Delaware lands to the English. Hatred between the Delaware and the Iroquois would last until the 1778 massacre in Pennsylvania's Wyoming Valley, a long-remembered land war in which the British and the Iroquois defeated Delawares and Connecticut settlers alleged to be squatters.

Although the French and British tried to enlist or buy the support of all tribes, the British were most successful among the eastern Iroquois, the French among the Seneca and Delaware. The Mohawk, closest to the crucial Montreal–New York waterway, were deeply divided between the Caughnawaga Mohawk near Montreal, who sided with the French, and the Hudson Valley Mohawk, who mostly sided with the British. By 1755, the two European powers had established two strong forts some 100 miles from each other: the French at Fort St. Frédéric (now Crown Point) on Lake Champlain, the British at Fort Edward on the Hudson River. In that year, however, the French decided to build a fort (Carillon, later called Ticonderoga) at the northern end of Lake George, and the British decided to build Fort William Henry at the southern end. It was a moment of historical collision when two expanding empires, built on differing concepts of land use, had advanced to either end of one lake. The proposal to build Fort William Henry was made by James De Lancey, the lieutenant governor of the province of New York, whose great-grandniece Susan Augusta De Lancey was to be the wife of James Fenimore Cooper.

When England, as everyone expected, officially declared war on France yet again, in May 1756, both nations redoubled their efforts to obtain Indian allies. William Johnson went to Onondaga for a two-week conference with the Six Nations, a meeting that ended in vague Iroquois pledges of support for the English. At his home, newly named Fort Johnson, Johnson also secured pledges of peace and possible support from the Shawanoe, some Delaware, and remnants of the scattered Mohegans. French general Montcalm was, however, at least as active. In preparing for the siege of Fort William Henry, he gathered at least 1,600 Indian allies from at least 30 tribes, including the Hurons, Abenakis, Ottawas, Miamis, Menomonies, and even the Iowas, many of them tribes displaced by Iroquois expansionism during the previous 100 years. There is evidence that the distant western tribes were fighting not primarily for revenge but because Montcalm promised them booty and the profit of selling prisoners. The war belt for the campaign was given, however, to the Caughnawaga Mohawk, who were contributing the most warriors (about 350) to the French cause.

To understand the interracial politics of Cooper's novel, the crucial historical fact is that, at the siege of Fort William Henry in 1757, most of the Iroquois were officially neutral, though mostly pro-British, while the Delaware were officially neutral, though mostly pro-French. (In 1755, the Delaware had fought with the French at the infamous defeat of British general Braddock.) In *The Last of the Mohicans*, however, these historical allegiances are reversed. Cooper repeatedly blurs the distinctions between the Hurons, the Six Nations, the divided Mohawk, and the Allegheny River Valley tribe called the Mingos, referring to them all rather vaguely as one nation, which is then portrayed as actively pro-French, rather than tacitly pro-British. Similarly, the distinction betwen Mohegan and Delaware is virtually erased, enabling Cooper to portray the Delaware chieftain Tamany, almost certainly dead in 1757, as a still living ancestor of Uncas, his fictional Mohican. More important, the pro-French sympaties of the historical Delaware are almost completely ignored. Chingachgook and Uncas, supposed descendants of Delaware as well as Mohican chiefs, are scouts and warriors who serve the British army. Cooper knew the historical truth of these allegiances, which was readily available in recently published accounts of the Delaware and the Iroquois written by John Heckewelder and De Witt Clinton. In the novel, Cooper passingly acknowledges that "by far the largest portion of his [Chingachgook's] nation were known to be in the field as allies of Montcalm" (224–25). Yet Cooper chose, in a novel contemptuous of "an imaginary and romantic picture of things, which never had any existence" (3), to alter known historical allegiances through character association.

The probable causes for these changes are more important than the details. There was, first of all, a pressing political reason for distorting the historical allegiances. In 1826, the French and Indian War was perceived from a post-Revolutionary perspective that viewed events prior to 1776 as seed-causes of the promising new Republic. During the American Revolution, four of the six Iroquois nations fought with the British; only the Tuscarora and the Oneida (the tribe near to Cooperstown) were to fight with the Americans. In 1777 and 1778, American troops were sent into the lands of the Mohawks, Onondagas, and Senecas to clear them of pro-British Indians hostile to the Revolution. Throughout the Revolutionary War, Joseph Brant's Mohawks (Magua is an adopted Mohawk), who had remained allies of the British, became the scourge of the New York frontier. By portraying the Iroquois of 1757 as actively pro-French, Cooper projects a Revolutionary War enemy back onto an earlier war, thus obtaining not a clear moral alignment of good versus evil but a clear historical alignment of winners versus losers. By focusing the reader's attention on the murderous hostility of the presumably pro-French Iroquois, Cooper tacitly justifies the eventual fate of the Six Nations. In historical fact, the division among the Six Nations over the Revolutionary War would not only end the League's neutrality; it would break the Six Nations openly apart into civil war. At the Battle of Fort Stanwix, Oneidas and Tuscaroras would fight openly against Mohawks and Senecas. By 1780, only 2 or 3 of the approximately 40 Iroquois towns were still habitable. In 1785, representatives of the Six Nations signed a treaty with the new U.S. government, agreeing to move their peoples to reservations within New York State. Cooper's 1831 introduction laments, "Of all the tribes named in these pages, there exist only a few half-civilized beings of the Oneidas, on the reservations of their people in New York. The rest have disappeared either from the regions in which their fathers dwelt, or altogether from the earth" (10). In fact, within New York state in 1831 there were four Iroquois reservations, with a total population of at least 5,000. In his desire to mourn racial decline, Cooper slighted a real and continuing, though much-reduced, Iroquois presence.

Personal reasons may also have prompted Cooper's shifting of tribal allegiances. William Cooper, the novelist's father, had acquired the extensive famly lands on Lake Otsego from creditors of George Croghan, the deputy of Sir William Johnson, who had received the land by treaty from Iroquois tribes in 1768. Unlike the Mohawks, the Oneidas had fought for the rebellious colonists during the Revolution. They would, however, fare none the better for it. In 1821, five years before *The Last of the Mohicans* was published, the Oneida lost many of their remaining lands to the Ogden Land Company through a virtually forced sale. In 1823, a large number of Oneidas began to remove to Wisconsin. By combining the Mohawks, Oneidas, Mingos, Hurons, and Iroquois into one seemingly pro-French and anti-progressive people, Cooper could elegize the powerless Delaware while displacing lingering guilt about family land title and the Oneidas' bleak future.

These explanations, however valid, may be less important than the fictional power of racial stereotyping. By blurring historical fact into a contrast between pro-English Delawares and pro-French Hurons, Cooper gave quintessential expression to the split image of the Indian in the white mind. His Delawares and Hurons readily absorb the doubled images of the Indian as epic hero (Achilles or Satan), as civilizable savage (Progressive or Red Stick), and as Natural Man (ingenuous or brutish). Because the imagined Indian has a doubled face, Cooper refers at least 20 times to the Delaware as a "people" or a "nation," even though by 1757 they were far more widely dispersed than the Iroquois, to whom Cooper rarely grants the status of a "nation." Although Cooper commonly uses the term *Indians* to refer to both Delaware and Iroquois, he applies the word *savage* 19 times to the satanic Magua but almost never to the Delaware.

For historical as well as literary reasons, Magua's tribal identity had to remain shadowy. Unless Magua is lying, he was born the son of a Huron chief but was exiled from his tribe after he was corrupted by the rum he first obtained from the French. Criticizing Colonel Munro's "imprudent severity" in whipping Magua for drunkenness is an effective, historically plausible means of preventing the reader from exonerating the British (118). Cooper would surely have been pleased to know that in 1756 Sir William Johnson had angrily warned Colonel Bagley, Colonel Monro's predecessor as commandant of Fort William Henry, that "Whenever any of them [Indian allies] get drunk the only way is to disarm them & tye them—& not to beat them."[11] Nonetheless, the implacable intensity and foul means of Magua's will to revenge have their own purpose in the novel's re-creation of political history. Magua's serving as a runner for the Mohawks who accompany the British forces (Magua/Maqua/Mohawk) is historically unlikely, but it is an effective way of associating the "savagery" of pro-French Hurons with the most visible and feared of Iroquois tribes at the time of the American Revolution.

However many liberties Cooper may have taken in his rendering of Indian life and allegiances, his portrayal of the fall of Fort William Henry remains balanced in its judgments and true to the known facts as recently presented in Ian Steele's careful, comprehensive history *Betrayals: Fort William Henry & The Massacre* (1990). Cooper conveys the isolation of forest roads and paths without forgetting that the newly built fort was in a crucial strategic location. Scouting parties combining friendly Indians and backwoodsmen without rank (e.g., Chingachgook, Uncas, and Hawkeye) had been a common and effective means of plundering, killing, scalping, spying on, and otherwise harassing the enemy all along the Lake Champlain frontier for years— as exemplified by the well-known Rogers Rangers. In 1756, two Mohicans were captured while fighting with Israel Putnam's Rangers; one of Montcalm's officers reported that he feared he could not prevent his Indian allies from making good on their threats to eat their two Mohican captives.

Although statistical guesses must always vary, Montcalm's besieging force of some 8,000 French regulars and Canadians, plus 1,600 Indians, vastly outnumbered Lieutenant Colonel George Monro's 2,000 to 3,000 troops, consisting of both English regulars and provincial militia, plus a small number of Indian allies. From the outset of the novel, Cooper conveys the importance of Montcalm's numerous and faceless Indian allies in heightening the terror of being besieged, both among the British regulars in the fort and among the very few troops sent to relieve it. Major Duncan Heyward is almost surely modeled on

Lieutenant Colonel John Young of the Sixtieth Royal Americans. Like Heyward, Young led a detachment of regulars from Fort Edward to the relief of Fort William Henry, 14 miles away, and then later assisted Monro in negotiating the terms of surrender. Cooper may somehow even have known that Monro's will left his money to three semi-anonymous and "reputed" children. Like any informed contemporary, Cooper surely did know that in 1777 Jane McCrea had left Fort Edward under Indian escort in order to join her beloved in Burgoyne's army, only to be scalped by pro-British Indians who were probably, like Magua, not members of another scouting party.

Cooper's portrayal of the character and conduct of the three principal historical figures is accurate and remarkably fair. Lieutenant Colonel Monro was, by all accounts, a brave and blunt commander who did everything possible to save his fort until the French intercepted a letter from Brigadier General Webb's subordinate informing Monro that Webb was declining to send the 3,000 troops that were available in Fort Edward and desperately needed as reinforcements. As soon as Monro knew that Webb's letter had been intercepted, Monro's surrender of his undermanned fort, with its exploded cannon, became both necessary and honorable. Although Cooper probably had not seen a copy of Webb's letter, Cooper's phrase "advised a speedy surrender" (186) is an accurate summary of it. Cooper portrays Munro as feeling "dishonour" and "shame" because Webb has "betrayed" him (186). In later historical accounts, however, the dishonor was to fall on General Webb himself; Webb's refusal to send reinforcements has seemed to all observers an act of self-protective vacillation, if not cowardice. In a different way from Chingachgook's grasping a British rifle or Munro's whipping of Magua, Webb's refusal to support his own troops prevents the reader from ascribing greater justice or gentlemanly honor to the British rather than the French cause.

In Cooper's fiction as in history, Montcalm grants Munro the most dignified conditions of surrender, allowing the British troops to retain their colors, their arms, and their possessions in exact accord with the highly complimentary terms of the eighteenth-century "parole of honor." It was Montcalm's apparent later violation of one of these terms—the British right to a safe escort after surrender—that allowed impulsive plundering to turn into random killing of disarmed British soldiers, their wives, and provincial recruits. The depositions of many a Massachusetts militiaman attest that Cooper is correct in portraying the French and French-Canadian soldiers as being able but unwilling to protect surrendered British soldiers and civilians from being defenselessly killed by the French army's own Indian allies. While the killing continues before the reader's eyes, Cooper tersely and correctly concludes only that "the armed columns of the Christian king stood fast, in an apathy which has never been explained" (202). By the careful pacing and central placement of this scene, the worst atrocity in Cooper's bloody book is revealed to be the moment when the forces of Christian civilization tacitly acquiesce in "savage" practices, violating an honorable agreement by doing nothing.

Cooper's characterization of the Marquis de Montcalm is historically plausible as well as symbolic. He is seen "in the zenith of his fortunes" (174) as the seeming epitome of "generous sentiments, high courtesy and chivalrous courage" (204). In the famous sentence in which Cooper charges the Marquis with "cruel apathy," we rightly sense an American democrat's suspicions of the superficial, compromised "chivalry" of the European aristocrat. But we should not forget that, by 1826, France was widely regarded, no longer so much as the losing enemy in the French and Indian War, but as the highly cultured libertarian nation whose alliance with the Americans had saved the Revolution.

On the one hand, Cooper's distrust of Montcalm leads him to ignore the valid claim that, once the killing had begun, Montcalm had personally done all he could to prevent further bloodshed. On the other hand, precisely because Cooper is a fair-minded historical novelist sensitive to the cross-currents of revolutionary allegiance, he does not, like many an American contemporary, villify Montcalm. The early morning meeting between Montcalm and Magua before the surrendering British march out of the fort is, on Montcalm's part, an encounter both unsought and unwelcome. Not only is Montcalm not a party to Magua's undisclosed plan for revenge; Montcalm physically prevents Magua from shooting Munro in cold blood. After Magua has departed, Cooper describes how Montcalm "lingered long and melancholy on the strand" (193), evidently trying to convince himself that Magua would not disregard European terms of surrender. These are not the responses of a treacherous hypocrite, but of a weak man who wishes to act honorably while closing his eyes to policies that are undoing his principles. The final charge Cooper levels at Montcalm is serious, restrained, and historically defensible: "he was deficient in that moral courage, without which no man can be truly great" (204). The quality of moral courage is, of course, exactly what General Webb lacks and Colonel Munro, to his own misfortune, possesses. If, however, the renowned historical figure who, above all other characters, epitomizes chivalry and culture is found to be lacking in "moral courage," then justifications of the spread of empire based on the true greatness of Euro-American civilization collapse.

Cooper's rendering of the "massacre"—the center of his novel's center—would continue to horrify and fascinate readers for at least a century. No reader can ever forget one provocative atrocity: a Huron, attracted by "the gaudy colors" of a British woman's shawl, seizes her baby, tries to exchange the baby for the shawl, and then, after failing to do so, "his bantering but sullen smile changing to a gleam of ferocity, he dashed the head of the infant against a rock, and cast its quivering remains to her very feet" (198). After the Huron murders the mother, Magua raises his "fatal and appalling whoop," provoking "two thousand raging savages" to descend out of the forest on defenseless white soldiers and families (199). In the immediate foreground of the massacre, Cooper thus places a sadistic, impulsive murder committed by a nameless "savage" against a nameless mother and child (198). Although the reader intellectually recognizes that the French soldiers are responsible for failing to stop the killing, the reader's visual attention is fixed on the savage's cruelty against mother and child in a way particularly resonant to nineteenth-century familial culture.

Incidents of exactly this kind had been reported in the most sensational of recent captivity narratives. Cooper may also have read a far more unrestrained account of the Fort William Henry massacre in the 1757 *New York Mercury*, an account claiming that infanticide had been real and continuing: "The Children were taken by the Heels and their Brains beat out against the Trees and Stones."[12] Whether such an incident ever occurred at Fort William Henry, however, would ultimately prove less important than Cooper's placing it there. From captivity narratives through film westerns, the image of the savage descending on the woman and her babe would out-Herod Herod in arousing horror at persecution of the innocent. For much of the nineteenth century, that image—which many would now see as blaming the victim—would be preserved on the steps of the U.S. Capitol building in Horatio Greenough's sculpture titled *The Rescue* (1837).

The power of the image of the greedy Huron, the woman with the shawl, and her battered child has often led readers to forget other and very different aspects of Cooper's account. The Huron's murder of mother and child is not the incident that causes the massacre to occur. In order for a single murder to have so inflammatory an effect, there has to have been a large group of French Indians who are near the retreating white women and ready to kill them. The Hurons' lust for blood has just been aroused by Magua, whom Cora suddenly sees "gliding among his countrymen, and speaking, with his fatal and artful eloquence" (198). But why are so many Hurons gathered in anger? An "avaricious" colonial militiaman has just left his ranks and tried to steal the plunder that Hurons believe is rightly theirs. As Cooper awkwardly puts it, "a truant provincial was paying the forefeit of his disobedience, by being plundered of those very effects, which had caused him to desert his place in the ranks" (197). Had this militiaman not been driven by a "savage" desire for plunder, neither the mood nor the occasion for the killings would have been present. Thus, the initial act provoking the massacre, as Cooper sees it, is to be traced back to the avarice of a colonist, and not to a Huron, Frenchman, or Englishman.

The issue of plunder that Cooper raises here is historically significant. Ian Steele argues with considerable plausibility that the Indians' killing of provincial and British soldiers was motivated not by bloodlust but by a frustrated desire for the booty, scalps, and prisoners that Montcalm had promised them as the fruits of victory. Prior to the scene of the massacre, Cooper has hinted at this possibility. When Magua meets Montcalm in the predawn, he expresses his contempt for the parole of honor by an angry rhetorical question: "What can the Hurons do? . . . Not a warrior has a scalp, and the pale faces make friends" (191). Moreover, Cooper senses that securing a profitable captive was probably as common a motive as killing for plunder. As the butchery ends, Cooper notes that "on every side the captured were flying before their relentless persecutors" (202); in the following narrative, our attention will be focused on the captives Magua has led away. In historical fact, more than 300 of the missing British and provincials who, according to early newspaper accounts, were assumed to have been murdered returned as captives and were redeemed by the English through the French at Halifax.

The horrid end of the surrender of Fort William Henry leaves, for all who confront it, troubling questions of degree and agency. Compared to his British historical sources, Cooper's novel is remarkably generous to Montcalm. Moreover, Cooper repeatedly qualifies, if not omits, the sensational accounts of Indian brutalities found in the depositions of the Massachusetts and New Hampshire provincials who had suffered most of the killing. Nonetheless, Cooper finally echoes Timothy Dwight in summarily referring to the event under "the merited title of 'the massacre of William Henry'" (204). What, then, constitutes a massacre? If we assume that a massacre is a substantial number of unprovoked killings, we must observe that, although Jonathan Carver believed there were 1,500 casualties, Cooper believed a more accurate figure would show that "between five and fifteen hundred" died "in this unhappy affair" (203, n.). After a close study of the incomplete and obviously unreliable historical record, Ian Steele concludes that the number killed could not have been less than 69 or more than 184, with some 500 more soldiers and civilians taken as captives. The lowest estimated percentage of those surrendered who were killed on 10 August 1757 would thus vary from about 40 percent (Jonathan Carver) to about 20 percent (Cooper) to about 3 percent (Steele). But if we accept the calculation that only 69 of 2,300 people were killed, should we then conclude that those 69 defenseless individuals were not "massacred?" Clearly, one person out of 2,300 does not a "massacre" make, but does 500? Does 69?

The use of such an inflammatory term as *massacre* surely depends more on cultural standards for conducting warfare than on numbers. If Montcalm promised his Indian allies scalps, prisoners, and plunder, and then agreed to a parole of honor that precluded his Indians from obtaining them, were those Indian allies who killed for scalps and plunder indulging in a massacre? Or were they insisting on obtaining their due through the only means now available to them? Could anyone who agrees with this last relativistic position possibly justify or even explain it to a family member of the slain, or to Colonel Monro? Through the voice of Magua, Cooper entertains this historical explanation for the murderous rage of Montcalm's Indians, but only fleetingly. Cooper's use of the word *massacre* in the context of this event ultimately depends on both his respect for the Judaeo-Christian commandment "Thou Shalt Not Kill" and his related respect for the integrity of the parole of honor. As a white author, Cooper can hint at a logical explanation for such brutal killing of disarmed people, but he cannot justify it. To associate unprovoked murder with red savagery, as Cooper does in rendering the massacre, is decidedly ethnocentric, but would not a determinedly multicultural perspective condone plunder, scalping, and abuse of prisoners? The equally important and less anachronistic charge may be disregard of alliance obligations. Cooper seems not to care whether or not his fictional Montcalm has explained the surrender terms to his Indian allies. The historical marquis had shown only slightly more concern; only after Montcalm and Monro had agreed to the parole of honor did Montcalm present it—as a fait accompli—to his Indian allies. Whether the 30-odd tribes speaking some 15 languages either understood or assented to the terms of surrender can never now be known.

History is, in the largest sense, the study of the consequences of the passage of time. Cooper's way of enlarging the stakes of his central historical event is to frame his account of the fort's surrender with two contrasted verbal paintings of the site, one before and one after the massacre. The evening after Cora and Alice arrive at the fort, Duncan Heyward ascends the ramparts of a bastion and looks out on Lake George:

The sun poured down his parting glory on the scene, without the oppression of those fierce rays that belong to the climate and the season. The mountains looked green, and fresh, and lovely; tempered with the milder light, or softened in shadow, as thin vapours floated between them and the sun. The numerous islands rested on the bosom of the Horican . . . in little hillocks of green velvet; among which the fishermen of the beleaguering army peacefully rowed their skiffs, or floated at rest on the glassy mirror, in quiet pursuit of their employment.

The scene was at once animated and still. All that pertained to nature was sweet, or simply grand; while those parts which depended on the temper and movements of man, were lively and playful.

Two little spotless flags were abroad, the one on a salient angle of the fort, and the other on the advanced battery of the besiegers; emblems of the truce which existed, not only to the acts, but it would seem, also, to the enmity of the combatants. Behind these, again, swung, heavily opening and closing in silken folds, the rival standards of England and France. (167–68)

The mood here is not simply one of peace, but of a foreboding, late afternoon tranquillity very like the opening page of Henry James's *The Portrait of a Lady*. As the gently moving waters form the sun's "glassy mirror," the green mountains and islands literally appear to have become Nature's bosom. The suspension of time, held in the calm moment of the late afternoon hour, complements the suspension of military and historical time decreed by the two political powers. Cooper's last paragraph implies, however, that Nature's tranquillity depends on the truce declared by human enemies. The "two little spotless flags" that announce the truce are soon displaced in Heyward's moving eye by the French and English flags that "swung, heavily, opening and closing in silken folds" (168). Nature's peace is feminine and life-giving, but its intensity depends on its seeming suspension from time. Had Heyward understood the landscape's inner signs, he would have predicted that the masculine world of war and politics was soon to enclose nature's "passing glory" in the heavy silken folds of two national flags.

On 13 August, after the victorious French have burned the fort and the "shrieks of the wounded and the yells of their murderers" (203) have died away, the five male protagonists return to the site of the massacre in search of Cora and Alice. This time, the landscape is seen through Cooper's eyes, not Heyward's. The author directs our attention not primarily to the "smoldering ruin" of the now useless fort but to the "change in season" that has occurred in just three intervening days:

> The sun had hid its warmth behind an impenetrable mass of vapour, and hundreds of human forms, which had blackened beneath the fierce heats of August, were stiffening in their deformity, before the blasts of a premature November. The curling and spotless mists, which had been seen sailing above the hills, towards the north, were now returning in an interminable dusky sheet, that was urged along by the fury of a tempest. The crowded mirror of the Horican was gone; and, in its place, the green and angry waters lashed the shores, as if indignantly casting back its impurities to the polluted strand. . . . Here and there, a dark green tuft rose in the midst of the desolation: the earliest fruits of a soil that had been fattened with human blood. The whole landscape, which, seen by a favouring light, and in a genial temperature, had been found so lovely, appeared now like some pictured allegory of life, in which objects were arrayed in their harshest but truest colours, and without the relief of any shadowing. (205)

Where all was clear and life-giving, all has now become impenetrable and deathly. Lake and land, polluted with the green fruits of red blood, lash out at each other in a seemingly futile effort to rid themselves of the perverse impurities that man has inflicted on them. The very quickness of the change from sultry August to premature November is itself a perversion, suggesting a human power over the natural cycle that works only for ill.

Perversions are supposed to be temporary. Cooper, however, insists that black corpses, angry waters, green tufts, and a premature November all make up a composite picture of the ultimate reality that Duncan Heyward had clearly wished to overlook. The perversions provide us with a "pictured allegory of life" in its "harshest but truest colours." Perversions, of course, must become permanent if the harshest colors are the most true. In the next paragraph, Cooper recognizes that continued contemplation of this nihilistic painting becomes intolerable. But when the eye seeks relief from life's harshest and truest colors, it does so "in vain, by attempting to pierce the illimitable void of heaven, which was shut to its gaze by the dusky sheet of ragged and driving vapour" (205). Cooper's diction has quietly heretical implications. Behind the driving vapor, the viewer's eye will be able to find only "the illimitable void of heaven." No God seems to have painted this particular allegory; the ultimate reality is the illimitable void.

This final and truest picture Cooper gives us of Lake George and Fort William Henry is one in which all corpses are indistinguishably black and no mention is made of French or British, provincial militia or European armies, Iroquois or Delaware, Hurons or Mohicans. It is a vision not unlike medieval allegory in which black-robed Death comes to Everyman, especially when Everyman is unprepared. But it is also a vision that contains the deepest historical meaning of Cooper's novel. The second allegorical view of the fort and its environs widens the significance of the summary remark Cooper had made on the Montreal–Albany waterway in his first chapter: "It became, emphatically, the bloody arena in which most of the battles for the mastery of the colonies were contested. Forts were erected at the different points that commanded the facilities of the route, and were taken and retaken, rased and rebuilt, as victory alighted on the hostile banners" (16). The novel's setting thus becomes a "bloody arena" (not merely an "area"), one encircling place of forced and inevitable combat where the succession of alternating victories amounts to no victory at all. No simple nationalist, Cooper has centered his novel around a humiliating defeat for Anglo-American forces, then rendered that defeat historically meaningless. After viewing the final state of the field of combat, we recognize that Munro and Montcalm have indeed staked life and honor "during the third year of a war which England and France last waged, for the possession of a country that neither was destined to retain" (17). Everywhere at Cooper's Fort William Henry, we feel the deathly waste created by men of both races who need to believe that their war-making must somehow be of permanent consequence.

INDIAN REMOVAL AND AMERICAN EMPIRE

Historical novelists who choose to write about an event they believe to be safely removed in time are likely to fill their novels with the customs and costumes of a quaintly bygone era. Because they do not allow past events to exert any pressure on the present, their novels sacrifice pertinence to periodicity, and end up indulging in an antiquarianism that can be of no lasting interest. *The Last of the Mohicans* is emphatically not this kind of historical fiction. Major concerns of the novel—white land hunger justified as the progress of civilization, the breaking up of red culture, and the inner price the white man pays for both—would become even more crucial in late nineteenth-century America than they had been in 1757. White settlement of the trans-Mississippi west, the major Indian wars, the development of the reservation system, the Dawes Severalty Act, and the steep decline in total Native American population—all these developments are latent in Cooper's novel but lie ahead of it in historical time. The immediate and lasting popularity of the novel must therefore be explained in contextual as well as intrinsic terms. Cooper published *The Last of the Mohicans* exactly at the time when the inflammatory and controversial issue of Indian Removal became acute. For readers in following decades, the fates of Cooper's Indians became a vehicle for the guilt as well as the self-justification that accompanied the spirit and the annexations of American Manifest Destiny.

By 1815, the Mohegans were virtually extinct, the Delaware had been removed to Ohio, and the Iroquois had been removed to reservations in New York, but most of the inland South was still held and inhabited by the Creek, Choctaw, Chickasaw, and Cherokee. White desire for the land of southern Indians and the Indians' frequent refusal to sell it had exposed, for the whole nation, problems of interracial policy that have never had a clear resolution. Are Indians

ave often seen the locust strip the leaves from the trees,
season of blossoms has always come again! (344–45)

view of white land hunger (whites as "locusts") is hardly
le from Magua's (whites as "hogs" and "wolves" [301]).
bes not predict the extinction of the red race; instead, he
pocalyptic going-off of the white man over the western
he rejuvenation of the red race during the blossoming of
is very last speech, the words that close the novel,
knowledges that "the pale-faces are masters of the earth"
ediately adds that "the time of the red-men has not yet
(394). "Not yet come again." To Tamenund there is,
protection for the red man anywhere to the west. The
ted wisdom, however, is to believe that the supposed
the red man may prove to be an illusion. If there is ulti-
he red man will flourish again as a natural consequence
han's wrongs. White proponents of Indian Removal, had
henund's words closely, would have found scant comfort

, gold was discovered on Cherokee land. The rapid
hite settlers only aggravated the removal issue, making
the Indian Removal Act seem even more necessary or
bus, depending on one's viewpoint. The crucial moment
uasion was Andrew Jackson's "First Annual Message,"
Congress in December 1829. Jackson presented the
al Act as a forced choice: either the Cherokee would
d the Mississippi or the laws of the state of Georgia
nded over them. In summing up why removal was the
protective, and honorably paternal of the two alterna-
resented a historical overview of red-white relations:

ors found them [the Indians] the uncontrolled posses-
regions. By persuasion and force they have been made
om river to river and from mountain to mountain, until
e tribes have become extinct and others have left but
to preserve for awhile their once terrible names.

separate and independent nations with whom the federal government makes treaties, or are Indians "domestic dependent peoples"—in effect, wards of the United States—for whom special protective policies must be devised? When a state enters the Union, does it have jurisdiction over Native American peoples living within its borders? If it does not, is white federal "protection" only a condescending ruse that permits continued dispossession of Indians in faraway locations? Is a treaty of land cession that is signed by one group of tribal chieftains (the so-called progressives) valid for the entire tribe or nation, including those who did not sign? Behind all these legal issues lay the dominant interracial question. Can whites and reds ever live together, or does proximity mean the extinction of the red man as well as red culture?

Sporadic wars and piecemeal land cessions between southern Indians and whites increased sharply after the Louisiana Purchase (1803) and continued almost unabated for the next 20 years. A comprehensive national policy for dealing with eastern Indians, first suggested by President Thomas Jefferson, was finally proposed to Congress by President James Monroe in 1825, the year before *The Last of the Mohicans* was published. Eventually passed under Democrat Andrew Jackson's administration in 1830, the controversial Indian Removal Act was promoted by a loose coalition of would-be planters, southern Democrats, southern state governors, and mid-Atlantic moderates. Removal was proposed as a humanitarian solution necessary for the protection of Indian culture and Indian lives. If the issue of the Indian's prior right of possession is set aside, the Act's provisions sound quite benign: a fair price for Indian lands, including improvements, was to be determined by the office of the Commissioner of Indian Affairs, then housed in the War Department. Tribes were then to be given, in perpetuity, an equal amount of land of comparable value across the Mississippi where they could live together unmolested by white traders and white land seekers. Indians would be protected on their westward journey by federal troops; the federal government would pay the expense of their journey and provide a one-year annuity to support Indians during resettlement.

For five years between the bill's proposal and its eventual passage, an equally loose coalition of Christian missionaries, northern Whigs, federal judges, and mid-Atlantic moderates protested that the Indian Removal Act was unjust as well as illegal. Such an act would violate long-standing land treaties that had been signed under War Department auspices with southern tribes as separate nations, treaties that had guaranteed those lands to southern tribes forever. Moreover, they argued, the Indian Removal Act was a high-sounding measure likely to be brutally and callously carried out. In reality, opponents said, Indian Removal was a way for politicians both to satisfy the land hunger of white frontiersmen and to rid their own states of persistent interracial friction. And finally, critics wondered, what would happen should Indian tribes refuse to exchange their lands? Would Indian Removal in fact be voluntary, as its proposers claimed, or would it not have to become compulsory?

Proponents of Indian Removal found it handy to write and speak of Indians as if they were all nomadic hunters, children of the forest irreclaimably committed to a tribal way of life that could not survive contact with white civilization. Hence, it proved acutely embarrassing that the Indians most opposed to being removed were the very ones who had most fully accepted white ways. As Cherokee John Ridge's "Essay on Cherokee Civilization" (1826) proudly proclaimed, the 14,000 citizens of "the Cherokee Nation" had their own National Council, a constitution, a court system, written laws, English newspapers and schools, farms with cattle and orchards, cotton plantations worked by 1,277 black slaves, and at least 200 interracial (red and white) married couples who owned private property.[13] President Jackson's constitutional response was to argue that the United States could not be a sovereign nation and that a state could not have secure rights were a separate nation allowed to exist within its boundaries. But the underlying cultural issue had already been fully planted in the public mind. The Cherokees' opposition to removal made it apparent that it was much too simple for whites to contend that, because the Indian could not adapt, he must be removed or face extinction.

In these contexts, how did the instant popularity of *The Last of the Mohicans* contribute to the controversy over the Indian Removal

Act? Readers predisposed to favor I
found their concept of the red man
slaveowning cotton planter—fully c
have fastened approvingly on those
suggest that the demise of the In
Cooper's closing chapters, domina
voice of Tamenund, implies that, i
ples have always been "scattered li
tices of the white man, however re
reader convinced of these beliefs v
gic about selected Mohegans who
vanished race, rather than to bed
recurrence of injustice. He or she
spirit: Be reminded of how satan
women and children at Fort Willi
let the epic regret of our nation
compromise!

The novel Cooper actually
gic nor so one-dimensional.
Americans—Montcalm, Munro,
tribute in major ways both to th
decimation of Indian cultures.
exults in the killing of any Ming
acter besides Alice who will not
and powerless as she.

Most important, the word
in fact express the resignation a
ciated with them. Tamenund
tribe, but not of the Indian
Tamenund says of the white m

I know that the pale-faces
that they claim, not only t
of their colour is better tha
let them not boast before t
entered the land at the ris

sun! I
but the

Tamenund's
distinguishab
Tamenund d
predicts an a
sunset, and t
spring. In h
Tamenund ac
but then imm
come again"
assuredly, no
most far-sig
extinction of
mate justice,
of the white
they read Tar
in them.

In 1828
increase of w
the passage o
more treacher
of public pers
spoken befor
Indian Remo
remove beyor
would be exte
more humane,
tives, Jackson

Our ances
sors of vas
to retire fr
some of th
remnants

> Surrounded by the whites with their arts of civilization, which by destroying the resources of the savage doom him to weakness and decay, the fate of the Mohegan, the Narragansett, and the Delaware is fast overtaking the Choctaw, the Cherokee, and the Creek. That this fate surely awaits them if they remain within the limits of the States does not admit of a doubt. Humanity and national honor demand that every effort should be made to avert so great a calamity. [14]

Through these words, Cooper's fictions have become a force in the formation of public policy. Andrew Jackson's selection of the Narragansett and the Delaware, to say nothing of the Mohegan, as the examples of America's nearly vanished tribes surely owes more to the immediate popularity of Cooper's *The Wept of Wish-ton-Wish* (a novel about Narragansett dispossession published earlier in 1829) and to *The Last of the Mohicans* than to any historical inquiry made by the president. Jackson clearly wishes Congress and the public to believe that passage of the Indian Removal Act will somehow prevent the Cherokee from becoming like the Mohicans. In fact, however, one of the few truths that no character in *The Last of the Mohicans* ever disputes is that forcing Indians westward has decimated them all. To James Fenimore Cooper, Uncas and Chingachgook may be the last of their tribe, but they are hardly the symbol of "savage . . . weakness and decay" that Jackson seeks to describe. Jackson's strategy is to appropriate Cooper's fiction by forgetting all its details in a glow of vague references and condescending paternal feeling; he makes adroit misuse of literature for effective political purpose.

When the Removal Act reached the floor of the House, the key speech in its favor was delivered by Representative Wilson Lumpkin, Democrat from Georgia. Lumpkin quoted in full Jackson's sentences about the Mohegan, the Narragansett, and the Delaware, describing Jackson's Annual Message as "the forcible language of truth, by your venerable Chief Magistrate."[15] But because Wilson Lumpkin, unlike Jackson, had no need to pose as the second Father of the entire nation, Lumpkin also took partisan occasion to lambast both missionaries and "Northern writers" whose pages are "filled with the sublimated cant of

the day" and whose readers will now "spend days and years in weeping over . . . the departure of the Cherokees from the bones of their
forefathers" (Lumpkin, 1087).

Despite some remarkable forensic denouncing of the hidden
compulsory aspect of the Removal Act (Whig congressman Edward
Everett of Massachusetts declared, "There, sir, I place my foot. It *is*
compulsory[16]), Jackson's Removal Act passed by a narrow margin.
Two years later, Wilson Lumpkin was to be elected governor of
Georgia, where he would help to ensure the signing of the treaty of
New Echota (1835), in which a minority of Cherokee chiefs, including
John Ridge, signed away their lands. Because many Cherokee still
refused to sign, to leave their lands, or to accept the laws of the state
of Georgia, it would soon be thought necessary to ensure compliance
with the Removal Act by having federal troops remove the Cherokee
physically. In 1838, Jackson's successor as president, Democrat Martin
Van Buren, ignoring a protest petition signed by 15,665 Indians, sent
federal troops under General Winfield Scott to Georgia to remove the
Cherokee. About 4,500 Cherokee, one-quarter of the remaining population, would die before the Cherokee Nation reached "Indian territory" in what is now Oklahoma.

In legal terms, the most infamous aspect of the "Trail of Tears"
was that Indian Removal had indeed become compulsory. President
Jefferson had insisted in 1809 that his policy would apply only to
"those who wish to remove."[17] President Monroe, introducing the
first removal bill to Congress, had acknowledged that "the removal of
the tribes from the territory which they now inhabit . . . should be
agreeable to themselves."[18] Even Andrew Jackson had assured con-
gressmen in his "First Annual Message" that "this emigration should
be voluntary, for it would be as cruel as unjust to compel the aborigines to abandon the graves of their fathers and seek a home in a distant
land" (Jackson 1829, 1:310). In that same year, Cooper addressed the
issue of Indian removal in *Notions of the Americans*. Arguing that
Indians who remain in contact with white civilization become "a stunt-
ed, dirty and degraded race," Cooper gave troubled, qualified approval
to voluntary removal, insisting at the same time that Indian disposses-

sion has historically been a "general and, in some degree justifiable, invasion of territory."[19] For reasons of tribal pride as well as place in historical time, compliance with forced removal would have been both unthinkable and utterly degrading to any Indian character in *The Last of the Mohicans.*

With the advantage of historical insight, we now knowingly protest against the cruel and futile consequences of Indian Removal. In this spirit, Cooper can also be charged not with ignoring the issue but with having such respect for the Indian heroic age that contemporary Indians seemed comparatively inconsequential and Indian Removal seemed a sad necessity. But one must be careful here. Lewis Cass, who argued strongly for voluntary Indian Removal in 1830, and who was to become Jackson's Secretary of War in 1832, was the same man who incurred Cooper's lifelong resentment by charging in 1828 that, while creating Uncas and Chingachgook, Cooper had "consulted the book of Mr. Heckewelder, instead of the book of nature."[20] Perhaps, too, we need to judge the policy of voluntary Indian removal from the perspective of the 1820s, as well as from that of the aftermath of its failure. Given the minuscule size of the federal government and the immensity of the frontier line, what exactly was the federal government to do when whites poured onto Indian lands? If there was a preferable and practicable alternative to voluntary Indian Removal honorably carried out, no one in Cooper's time (and perhaps now as well) seems to have known precisely what it was.

The Last of the Mohicans laments the end of the Indian heroic age in human history, but it does not justify it. Such a lament seemed inevitable in terms of the white man's historical understanding, but not in terms of the Indian's understanding of the future. The novel has been used, by Parkman and Simms among others, to predict the unstoppable extinction of the red race, but the words of Cooper's text do not support this conclusion. Cooper's affirmations of the westward course of empire are always uneasy, undermined by his guilt over the worth and the rights of those who have been effaced. Surely the dominant mood of the novel, if it has one, is a spirit of emotional protest against the continuing decimation of red tribes, and the white man's complicity in the process. It is this mood—one that can be called ele-giac denunciation—that Andrew Jackson so resented. In December 1830, speaking again to Congress, but now after the passage of the Indian Removal Act, Jackson indulged in a flourish of triumph:

> Humanity has often wept over the fate of the aborigines of this country, and Philanthropy has been long busily employed in devising means to avert it, but its progress has never for a moment been arrested, and one by one have many powerful tribes disap-peared from the earth. To follow to the tomb the last of his race and to tread on the graves of extinct nations excite melancholy reflections. But true philanthropy reconciles the mind to these vicissitudes as it does to the extinction of one generation to make room for another.[21]

To Jackson, "true philanthropy" is a habit of mind that accepts the racial "extinction" that must always demonstrate civilization's progress. Mourning over the tomb of an Uncas, last of his race, thus becomes a phony humanity, unworthy of a true citizen.

Warming to the promise of conquered frontiers, Jackson then declares his contempt for all the complainers by defining phony phil-anthropy:

> Philanthropy could not wish to see this continent restored to the condition in which it was found by our forefathers. What good man would prefer a country covered with forests and ranged by a few thousand savages to our extensive Republic, studded with cities, towns and prosperous farms, embellished with all the improvements which art can devise or industry execute, occupied by more than 12,000,000 happy people, and filled with all the blessings of liberty, civilization, and religion? (Jackson 1830, 1:335)

In Jackson's words we sense the exasperation of many an influential contemporary who honestly could not understand why the felling of the forest and the dying out of the savage were legitimate causes for regret. Jackson's rhetorical question could be aimed at admiring read-ers of *The Last of the Mohicans* who, after initially being told of the "inroads of civilization" (7), were promptly immersed in an eighteenth-century forest and ultimately asked to mourn for the long-dead chiefs of a minor tribe. But President Jackson's rhetorical question expresses the pride of the victor as well as the genuine incredulity of the man—a smugness in statistical domination, and a refusal to consider that "liberty, civilization, and religion" could bring anything but "blessings." By spreading the American eagle over "this continent," Jackson's "Second Annual Message" proved to be exactly the kind of speech against which Tamenund had warned: "But let them not boast before the face of the Manitto too loud" (345).

7

Epilogue: To Kill or Not to Kill

When at age 60 Cooper wrote a comprehensive preface for the five Leatherstocking Tales, he looked back on Natty Bumppo, their gradually emerging central figure, as a hero who had combined the best qualities of both races:

> In a moral sense this man of the forest is purely a creation. The idea of delineating a character that possessed little of civilization but its highest principles as they are exhibited in the uneducated, and all of savage life, that is not incompatible with these great rules of conduct, is perhaps natural to the situation in which Natty is placed. . . . Removed from nearly all the temptations of civilized life, placed in the best associations of that which is deemed savage, and favorably disposed by nature to improve such advantages, it appeared to the writer that his hero was a fit subject to represent the better qualities of both conditions, without pushing either to extremes. (396–97)

Leatherstocking's moral courage and variable "gifts," like his biracial clothing and reddened skin, attest to his imagined identity as man on the cultural margin, able to assimilate the best qualities of both races.

For the older Cooper as for many a reader, Leatherstocking has become the ideal frontiersman, whose unfailing prowess is somehow attributable to his inner integrity and to his ability to see God in the forest, hear Him in the winds, and bow to Him "in the firmament that o'ercanopies all" (397).

For the careful reader of *The Last of the Mohicans*, there are many problems in such an attractive formulation. Above the killing fields of Fort William Henry, we see "the illimitable void of heaven" (205), not God in His firmament. The forest is too all-enclosing, and the scout is usually too busy, for Hawkeye to engage in many discourses on Nature's beneficence. At the most crucial moment of historical action, the siege and massacre at the fort, Hawkeye's virtues are locked up in a French prison. If Leatherstocking is to be remembered as the best of both races, why does he repeatedly insist that he is a "man without a cross"? Does Hawkeye choose to be on the margin, or has he been marginalized by cultures not worthy of him? And most important, what exactly are "these great rules of conduct," these "highest principles," which, Cooper affirms, have set civilization above the "savage life"?

There was much culturally invested in this last question. The removal and destruction of Indian cultures were repeatedly defended by Cooper's contemporaries on the grounds that Christian civilization, precisely because it was merciful and humane, had every right to supplant the spiritual barbarism of the red man. Indians, it was commonly assumed, were still living by tribal practice of the Old Law: the *Lex Talionis*, an eye for an eye, kill or be killed. Thankfully, however, the great Christian "rules of conduct," the white man's "highest principles," were spreading across the continent the New Law: love your neighbor as yourself; do unto others as you would have others do unto you; blessed are the merciful, for they shall obtain mercy.

For Cooper's contemporaries, the vexing problem faced by every intellectually honest white person who thought about the westward-moving frontier was the question of means. If a Christian frontiersman reverts to savage practices to gain savage lands, is he still a Christian? But if he is not willing to shoot first and ask later, can he survive? In situations where Indians were unwilling to defer to Christian morality, how much force should whites be willing to use in order to bring about progress? A bleak prospect threatened: if the forests could be cleared only by savage means, then American pioneers would have brought to the State of Nature, not Christian civilization but a merely technological progress driven by the Old Law rather than the New.

In four of the five Leatherstocking Tales, Natty Bumppo fleetingly mentions that he was raised among the Moravians. Natty's earliest upbringing, easily overlooked by scholars because he himself wishes to slight it, in fact proves to be no idle detail. The Moravians were a Reformation Protestant sect, many of whom came from Germany to Georgia and Pennsylvania in the 1730s and 1740s in order to convert the Indians. Centered in Bethlehem, Pennsylvania, near the Delaware River, the Moravians taught Mohawk to their children and by 1750 had at least 50 missionaries among the Iroquois, the Delaware, and among remnants of the Mohegans at Skeksmeter, New York, and Stockbridge, Massachusetts. Moravian missions among the Cherokee of Georgia would fare well until the 1820s, when the Moravians' concerted opposition to Indian Removal caused a swift decline in influence. For the young Nathaniel Bumppo, however, the important fact was that the Moravians had founded nonseparating communities in the hope that they might live by Christian law, and might persuade Indians to do the same. Following their founder, Count Zinzendorf, Moravians were pacifists who believed that the New Testament words of Jesus Christ (the only Man-God in history) were the sole, absolute, and literal source of God's Truth. In the Sermon on the Mount, Moravians had read of how Christ had made Jehovah's absolute sixth commandment "Thou Shalt Not Kill" even more astringent: "You have heard that it was said to the men of old, 'you shall not kill; and whoever kills shall be liable to judgment.' But I say to you that every one who is angry with his brother shall be liable to judgment" (Matthew 5:21–22). Consequently, during both the American Revolution and the French and Indian War, the Moravians persistently refused to take up arms on either side.

If "Christian conquest" is a contradiction in terms, then endowing Leatherstocking with a Moravian upbringing only compounds the problem of praising a hero who kills. Natty Bumppo has good reason to gloss over his Moravian years. When we first see Hawkeye, he has served with William Johnson's army and is at present a scout for Major Effingham's British forces. Cooper's opening description centers upon the quality that has given him his Indian name: "The eye of the hunter, or scout, whichever he might be, was small, quick, keen, and restless, roving while he spoke on every side of him, as if in quest of game, or distrusting the sudden approach of some possibly lurking enemy. Notwithstanding these symptoms of habitual suspicion, his countenance was not only without guile, but at the moment at which he is introduced, it was charged with an expression of sturdy honesty" (36). To be Hawkeye evidently involves more than sharpness of vision; one must be always and relentlessly on the lookout either for one's enemy or one's game. This impression of the scout's combative outlook is immediately countered, however, by a sentence that ascribes to Hawkeye's face an engaging honesty that seems more than momentary. Clearly, Cooper will try to have it both ways; his hero will somehow be a hawk without guile, a predator only by necessity.

When Hawkeye first sees Magua, his instinct rightly tells him he has met a mortal enemy. Hawkeye's immediate wish is to shoot the unsuspecting Magua "between the ankle and the knee" (47), thereby disabling him for at least a month until Munro's daughters arrive at the fort and the siege is concluded. Hawkeye is dissuaded from this most unchristian stratagem, not by the voice of inner conscience, but by Duncan Heyward, who twice protests that "it will not do. He may be innocent" (47) immediately after Hawkeye has twice raised his rifle. Upon first reading this passage, we are likely to agree with Heyward that shooting an unknown and unsuspecting man in cold blood is indefensible. In retrospect, after we have heard Magua's repeated war cry, followed his abductions of Cora, and seen his back-stabbing murder of Uncas, we may wonder whether Hawkeye's strategy would not have been more humane as well as more wise. It is Heyward's advice, not Magua's motive, that will prove to be deadly "innocent."

While Hawkeye condemns Magua as a Mingo devil, he also insists that implacable revenge is an Indian's "gift," a long-standing racial practice not to be judged by white standards. Hawkeye struggles to be open-minded—and thereby to honor his own "red" virtues—

while still remaining "a man without a cross." Hawkeye's pointed ridicule of David Gamut's belief that his Bible will protect him is Cooper's way of showing that Christian ethics are simply not practicable on any frontier, let alone a war-torn forest. But Hawkeye's need to mock Gamut is also of a piece with his need to display his beliefs that words in any book are but "black marks" on a page (37), and that the only book he has ever read, the only book worth reading, is the book of Nature, not the Bible (134). Such statements are guilt-driven instances of protesting too much. As Hawkeye listens unobserved to David Gamut singing the "low, dying chords" of a hymn, "his roving eyes began to moisten, and before the hymn was ended, scalding tears rolled out of fountains that had long seemed dry, and followed each other down those cheeks that had oftener felt the storms of heaven, than any testimonials of weakness" (68–69). The "low, dying chords" of David's hymn elicit from Hawkeye regret for a lost life and lost values that can derive only from his years among the Moravians, who were as famous for hymn singing as any Connecticut psalmodist. Whether it is Cooper or Hawkeye who regards these tears as "testimonials of weakness" is, however, impossible to say.

During the Huron attack at Glenn's Falls, an elaborate incident of suspended melodrama reveals Hawkeye's conflicting inner ethics about killing. Ambushed by a Huron shooting down from an oak tree, Hawkeye and the Mohicans fire simultaneously, wounding the Huron so that he slips from the tree and dangles over the precipice, holding onto a branch. Cooper then leaves "the wretch" dangling from that branch for six paragraphs while Hawkeye considers whether to waste a precious bullet and powder on an enemy who is sure to die. Once again, it is Duncan Heyward who speaks for Christian mercy—"Give him, in pity, give him the contents of another rifle" (86)—and Hawkeye who speaks for practical necessity: "'tis their scalps, or ours!" (86). Once again, the Christian upbringing of the man without a cross momentarily prevails: after raising his rifle three times "in mercy" and then lowering it, Hawkeye finally shoots the tormented Huron just as he loses his struggle to retain his handhold. This time, however, Leatherstocking makes the folly of mercy explicit to the reader: "'Twas the last charge in my horn, and the last bullet in my pouch, and 'twas the act of a boy! . . . what mattered it whether he struck the rock living or dead!" (87).

Although this scene has acquired a comic familiarity, it lingers troublingly in the mind. The white hero who supposedly embodies civilization's "highest principles" rightly regrets practicing the blessedness of mercy, even in the form of a bullet. Throughout the rest of the novel, Cooper will immerse the reader in the consequences of Hawkeye's moral practicality. After Magua has escaped from a battlefield full of dead Hurons, "the honest but implacable scout made the circuit of the dead into whose senseless bosoms he thrust his long knife, with as much coolness, as though they had been so many brute carcasses" (131). When he recalls his first battle, he regrets having wasted time burying the Mohawk dead, remarking, "Yes, yes: I was then young, and new to the sight of blood, and not relishing the thought that creatures who had spirits like myself, should lay on the naked ground" (143). Now, however, Hawkeye does relish that thought, proclaiming "with an air of military pride" that there is not "the space of a square mile atwixt Horican and the river, that 'kill-deer' hasn't dropped a living body on" (154). When Chingachgook returns from an ambush, carrying the "reeking scalp" of a French sentinel, Hawkeye is thoughtful but not disapproving, noting that scalping is, after all, an Indian's gift, and regretting only that it was a Frenchman who has been scalped, rather than "an accursed Mingo" (156). Hawkeye will later discouragingly remark, "God knows what the country would be, if the settlements should ever spread far from the two rivers. Both hunting and war would lose their beauty" (239). To appreciate the beauties of war has become, Cooper insists, the essence of Hawkeye's inner being: "that secret love of desperate adventure . . . had increased with his experience, until hazard and danger had become, in great measure, necessary to the enjoyment of his existence" (259).

The hardened scout has come to know that, on the frontier, preventive killing is a necessity. If he and the Mohicans are to protect white women, white officers, and a Christian psalmodist, they must at the appropriate moment tell lies, kill pack animals, fire the first bullet, and scalp or stab men whom they have felled. For success and for survival, Hawkeye has found that "do unto others as you would have others do unto you" must in daily practice become "do, lest you be done by."

Hawkeye's "secret love of desperate adventure" has, however, made him reluctant even to admit to his own bloody compromise with the Christian's Golden Rule. He often rationalizes his compromise by insisting that, because revenge is an Indian and not a white code, he will practice it only as a momentary exception. When Hawkeye looks out over the blackening corpses near the smoldering fort, he vows eternal revenge against the French and their Indians, but he prefaces his vow by insisting, "Revenge is an Indian feeling, and all who know me, know that there is no cross in my veins; but this much I will say . . ." (208). Here the word indicating an exception (*but*) actually introduces a guiding rule. In a climactic scene recalling Hawkeye's earlier shooting of the Indian in the tree, Hawkeye finally kills Magua by shooting him as he clings to a shrub atop a cliff. This time, however, there is no reluctance: "The form of Hawk-eye had crouched like a beast about to take its spring, and his frame trembled so violently with eagerness, that the muzzle of the half raised rifle played like a leaf fluttering in the wind" (381). Revenge, however justified it may be, has here made Hawkeye appear at least momentarily bestial. Ironically, images of bestiality have been applied throughout the novel to denigrate the very "savage" whom Hawkeye is now so eagerly and triumphantly killing.

The disillusioned and bloody-minded scout little resembles Leatherstocking's later reincarnation as Pathfinder, a romantic hero whose love for Nature's God, like his love for one woman, leads Cooper to describe him as "a sort of type of what Adam might have been supposed to be before the fall, though certainly not without sin."[22] Hawkeye's only recognizably Adamic quality, it seems, is his reluctance to think about the spiritual consequences of disobeying God's commandment. Only at one moment in Cooper's narrative does Hawkeye directly confront his compromising of Christian ethics. After Hawkeye swears that, should David Gamut be scalped, he and Uncas will swiftly take revenge "as becomes true warriors and trusty friends" (310), David bursts out in protest, asking Hawkeye to "forgive my destroyers" because "I am an unworthy and humble follower of one, who taught not the damnable principle of revenge" (310).

Because the word *damnable* still meant "capable of damning one to an eternity in Hell," Cooper's hero is brought up short. How is Hawkeye—a killer raised a Moravian—to reply?:

> The scout hesitated, and appeared to muse.
> "There is a principle in that," he said, "different from the law of the woods! and yet it is fair and noble to reflect upon!" Then, heaving a heavy sigh, probably among the last he ever drew in pining for the condition he had so long abandoned, he added—"it is what I would wish to practyse myself, as one without a cross of blood, though it is not always easy to deal with an Indian, as you would with a fellow christian. God bless you, friend; I do believe your scent is not greatly wrong, when the matter is duly considered, and keeping eternity before the eyes, though much depends on the natural gifts, and the force of temptation." (310)

An engaging, even a touching, admission, written with an ear for Leatherstocking's mispronounciations ("practyse"), his slangy metaphors ("scent"), and the run-on quality of speech that reinforces his honesty. But Hawkeye's winning frankness leads to no resolution of the issue. Because Hawkeye heaves a "heavy sigh" for having knowingly "abandoned" principles of mercy, his claim still to be a "fellow christian" can be only a wistful rationalization. "Fellow white" would be the more accurate phrase for "a man without a cross" now living by red codes of revenge. Evidently hoping to refute David Gamut, Hawkeye begins these musings with a confident assertion but soon breaks down into hesitant qualifications that reflect his vacillating between absolute and race-relative standards. Although Hawkeye is still concerned about "keeping eternity before the eyes," Cooper tells us that Hawkeye's heavy sigh is "probably the last he ever drew" for all he has lost. His final words convey only the muted hope that "the force of temptation" might perhaps justify the Indian practices for which he feels only half-guilty.

The Last of the Mohicans shows us that even the most admirable white frontiersman will learn to initiate preventive and retaliatory killing. Moreover, he will learn to justify and sometimes to enjoy it. A few Indians like Uncas may share the white man's feelings, but many more whites will practice the very barbarities they condemn as savagery. The conquering of the wilderness forces New World Christians to act like Old World pagans. Just as the distinction between red and white cultures disappears in the characterization of Leatherstocking, so the lines separating red and white races, despite Cooper's conscious desire to keep them drawn, are forever being blurred and erased. As a Yale-educated white author whose father's lands had recently belonged to the Iroquois, Cooper could not but hope that the westward course of empire would mean the spread of civilization, of Christianity, and therefore of Progress. Without abandoning the hope embedded in these powerful clichés, he vividly imagined America's repeated failure to realize them. Precisely because white Euro-American cultures would become so dominant, such an author remains worth our reading time. Among the ironies of condescending to Cooper has been the belief, periodically reinforced by film versions of *The Last of the Mohicans*, that Cooper gladly indulges in an especially American love for gratuitous violence. In fact, the futilely suppressed signs of white savagery, from Magua's bloodied body to Hawkeye's bloodied soul, are felt on almost every page.

Notes and References

1. See the discussions of the phrase "identity politics" by Paul Berman and Edward W. Said in *Debating P.C.: The Controversy over Political Correctness on College Campuses*, ed. Paul Berman (New York: Dell Publishing Group, 1992), 13, 177.

2. George Dekker and John P. McWilliams, eds., *Fenimore Cooper: The Critical Heritage* (London and Boston: Routledge & Kegan Paul, 1973), 60, 62; hereafter cited in text by page number only.

3. D. H. Lawrence, *Studies in Classic American Literature* (1923) (New York: Penguin Books, 1977), 7; hereafter cited in text by page number only.

4. Walter Scott, *Journal*, 14 March 1826, quoted in Jane Austen: *The Critical Heritage*, ed. B. C. Southam (London: Routledge & Kegan Paul, 1968), 106.

5. James Fenimore Cooper, "Review of Lockhart's Life of Scott," *Knickerbocker* 2 (1838): 363–64.

6. Roy Harvey Pearce, *Savagism and Civilization* (Berkeley: University of California Press, 1988), 51.

7. Dee Brown, *Bury My Heart at Wounded Knee* (New York: Henry Holt, 1970), 170, 172.

8. Thomas Jefferson, *Notes on the State of Virginia* (1784), in *The Portable Thomas Jefferson*, ed. Merrill D. Peterson (New York: Penguin, 1977), 96.

9. Catharine Maria Sedgwick, *Hope Leslie; or, Early Times in the Massachusetts*, ed. Mary Kelley (New Brunswick, N.J.: Rutgers University Press, 1987), 81; hereafter cited in text.

10. Lydia Maria Child, *Hobomok & Other Writings on Indians* (1824), ed. Carolyn L. Karcher (New Brunswick, N.J.: Rutgers University Press, 1986), 6; hereafter cited in text.

11. Quoted in Ian K. Steele, *Betrayals: Fort William Henry & the "Massacre"* (New York and Oxford: Oxford University Press, 1990), 71.

12. *New-York Mercury*, 22 August 1757, n.p.

13. John Ridge, "Essay on Cherokee Civilization" (1826), in *The Harper American Literature*, ed. Donald McQuade et al. (New York: Harper & Row, 1987), 1:730–31.

14. Andrew Jackson, "First Annual Message," delivered to Congress December 1829, in *The State of the Union Messages of the Presidents, 1790–1966*, ed. Fred L. Israel, introduction by Arthur M. Schlesinger (New York: Chelsea House, 1966), 1:309; hereafter cited in text as Jackson 1829.

15. Wilson Lumpkin, "Speech on the Indian Removal Bill," 6 May 1830, in *The American Indian and the United States: A Documentary History*, ed. Wilcomb E. Washburn (New York: Random House, 1973), 2:1083; hereafter cited in text as Lumpkin.

16. Edward Everett, "Speech in Opposition to the Indian Removal Bill," 28 May 1830, in *Speeches on the Bill for the Removal of the Indians* (Boston: Perkins & Marvin, 1830), 298.

17. Thomas Jefferson, "Preamble to the Cherokee Treaty" (1817), in *The American Indian and the United States*, ed. Washburn, 2:1073.

18. James Monroe, "Message to Congress," 27 January 1825 in *The American Indian and the United States*, ed. Washburn, 2:1075.

19. James Fenimore Cooper, *Notions of the Americans* (1828), ed. Robert E. Spiller (New York: Frederick Ungar, 1963), 2:277.

20. Lewis Cass, "Indians of North America," *North American Review* 22 (July 1826): 67.

21. Andrew Jackson, "Second Annual Message," delivered to Congress, December 1830, in *The State of the Union Messages of the Presidents*, ed. Israel, 1:335; hereafter cited in text as Jackson 1830.

22. James Fenimore Cooper, *The Pathfinder; or, The Inland Sea* (1840), ed. Richard D. Rust (Albany: State University of New York Press, 1981), 134.

Selected Bibliography

Primary Works

Works by Cooper

Beard, James F., ed. *The Letters and Journals of James Fenimore Cooper*. 6 vols. Cambridge, Mass.: Harvard University Press, 1960–68.

Cooper, James Fenimore. *Cooper's Novels*. 32 vols. Illustrated from drawings by F. O. C. Darley. New York: W. A. Townsend, 1861.

———. *Notions of the Americans* (1828). 2 vols. New York: Frederick Ungar, 1963.

Readily Available Reprints of the Leatherstocking Tales

The Deerslayer (1841). Edited by H. Daniel Peck. Oxford: Oxford University Press, 1993.

The Last of the Mohicans (1826). Edited by John McWilliams. Oxford: Oxford University Press, 1994.

The Pathfinder (1840). Edited by William P. Kelly. Oxford: Oxford University Press, 1993.

The Pioneers (1823). Edited by James D. Wallace. Oxford: Oxford University Press, 1992.

The Prairie (1827). Edited by Donald A. Ringe. Oxford: Oxford University Press, 1992.

Works by Other Writers

Carver, Jonathan. *Travels through the Interior Parts of North America in the Years 1766, 1767, and 1768* (1781). Minneapolis: Rosso Haines, 1956.

Cass, Lewis. "Indians of North America." *North American Review* 22 (July 1826):53–119.

———. "Removal of the Indians." *North American Review* 30 (October 1830):62–121.

Child, Lydia Maria. *Hobomok & Other Writings on Indians*. Edited by Carolyn L. Karcher. New Brunswick, N.J.: Rutgers University Press, 1986.

Dwight, Timothy. *Travels in New England and New York* (1821). Cambridge, Mass.: Belknap Press of Harvard University Press, 1969.

Everett, Edward. "Speech on the Indian Removal Bill." In *Speeches on the Bill for the Removal of the Indians*. Boston: Perkins & Marvin, 1830.

Jackson, Andrew. "First Annual Message Delivered to Congress" (1829) and "Second Annual Message Delivered to Congress" (1830). In *The State of the Union Messages of the Presidents*, vol. 1. Introduction by Arthur M. Schlesinger. New York: Chelsea House, 1966.

Lumpkin, Wilson. "Speech on the Indian Removal Bill." In *The American Indian and the United States: A Documentary History*, vol. 2. Edited by Wilcomb E. Washburn. New York: Random House, 1973.

Milton, John. *Paradise Lost* (1667). Edited by Scott Elledge. New York: W. W. Norton, 1975.

Ridge, John. "Essay on Cherokee Civilization" (1826). In *The Harper American Literature*, vol. 1. Edited by Donald McQuade, Robert Atwan, Martha Banta, Justin Kaplan, David Mintner, Cecelia Tichi, and Helen Vendler. New York: Harper & Row, 1987.

Scott, Walter. *Waverley; or, Sixty Years Since*. New York and London: Viking Penguin, 1988.

Sedgwick, Catharine Maria. *Hope Leslie; or, Early Times in the Massachusetts*. Edited by Mary Kelley. New Brunswick, N.J.: Rutgers University Press, 1987.

Secondary Works

Books on Cooper and His Novels

Dekker, George. *James Fenimore Cooper: The American Scott*. New York: Barnes & Noble, 1967.

Dekker, George, and John P. McWilliams, eds. *Fenimore Cooper: The Critical Heritage*. London: Routledge & Kegan Paul, 1973.

Franklin, Wayne. *The New World of James Fenimore Cooper*. Chicago: University of Chicago Press, 1982.

Grossman, James. *James Fenimore Cooper*. Stanford, Calif.: Stanford University Press, 1967.

House, Kay Seymour. *Cooper's Americans*. Columbus: Ohio State University Press, 1965.

Kelly, William P. *Plotting America's Past: Fenimore Cooper and the Leatherstocking Tales*. Carbondale: Southern Illinois University Press, 1983.

McWilliams, John P., Jr. *Political Justice in a Republic: James Fenimore Cooper's America*. Berkeley: University of California Press, 1972.

Motley, Warren. *The American Abraham*. New York: Cambridge University Press, 1987.

Nevius, Blake. *Cooper's Landscapes: An Essay on the Picturesque Vision*. Berkeley: University of California Press, 1976.

Peck, H. Daniel. *A World By Itself: The Pastoral Moment in Cooper's Fiction*. New Haven, Conn.: Yale University Press, 1977.

Railton, Stephen. *Fenimore Cooper: A Study of His Life and Imagination*. Princeton, N.J.: Princeton University Press, 1978.

Rans, Geoffrey. *Cooper's Leather-Stocking Novels: A Secular Reading*. Chapel Hill: University of North Carolina Press, 1991.

Ringe, Donald A. *James Fenimore Cooper*. New Haven, Conn.: College and University Press, 1962.

Wallace, James D. *Early Cooper and His Audience*. New York: Columbia University Press, 1986.

Cooper's Place in American Literature

Barnett, Louise K. *The Ignoble Savage: American Literary Racism, 1790–1890*. Westport, Conn.: Greenwood Press, 1975.

Berkhofer, Robert. *The White Man's Indian*. New York: Alfred A. Knopf, 1978.

Bewley, Marius. *The Eccentric Design: Form in the Classic American Novel*. London: Chatto & Windus, 1959.

Chase, Richard. *The American Novel and Its Tradition*. Rev. ed. Baltimore, Md.: Johns Hopkins University Press, 1980.

Dekker, George. *The American Historical Romance*. Cambridge, England: Cambridge University Press, 1987.

Fiedler, Leslie A. *Love and Death in the American Novel*. New York: Criterion, 1960.

Fisher, Philip. *Hard Facts: Setting and Form in the American Novel*. New York: Oxford University Press, 1985.

Kolodny, Annette. *The Lay of the Land*. Chapel Hill: University of North Carolina Press, 1975.

Lewis, R. W. B. *The American Adam: Innocence, Tragedy, and Tradition in the Nineteenth Century*. Chicago: University of Chicago Press, 1955.

McWilliams, John P., Jr. *The American Epic 1770–1860: Transforming a Genre*. Cambridge, England: Cambridge University Press, 1989.

Pearce, Roy Harvey. *Savagism and Civilization*. Rev. ed. Baltimore, Md.: Johns Hopkins University Press, 1965.

Porte, Joel. *The Romance in America*. Middletown, Conn.: Wesleyan University Press, 1969.

Ringe, Donald A. *The Pictorial Mode: Space and Time in the Art of Bryant, Irving, and Cooper*. Lexington: University of Kentucky Press, 1971.

Slotkin, Richard. *Regeneration Through Violence*. Middletown, Conn.: Wesleyan University Press, 1973.

Smith, Henry Nash. *Virgin Land: The American West as Symbol and Myth*. New York: Vintage, 1950.

Tompkins, Jane. *Sensational Designs: The Cultural Work of American Fiction, 1790–1860*. New York: Oxford University Press, 1985.

Essays on *The Last of the Mohicans*

Baym, Nina. "The Women of Cooper's Leatherstocking Tales." *American Quarterly* 23 (December 1971): 696–709

Beard, James F. Afterword to *The Last of the Mohicans*. New York: New American Library, 1962.

Blakemore, Steven. "Strange Tongues: Cooper's Fiction of Language in *The Last of the Mohicans*." *Early American Literature* 19 (Spring 1984): 21–44.

Butler, Michael D. "Narrative Structure and Historical Process in *The Last of the Mohicans*." *American Literature* 48 (May 1976): 117–39.

Darnell, Donald. "Uncas as Hero: The Ubi Sunt Formula in *The Last of the Mohicans*." *American Literature* 37 (November 1965): 259–66.

French, David P. "James Fenimore Cooper and Fort William Henry." *American Literature* 32 (March 1960): 28–38.

Haberly, David T. "Women and Indians: *The Last of the Mohicans* and the Captivity Tradition." *American Quarterly* 28 (Fall 1976): 431–43.

McWilliams, John. "Red Satan: Cooper and the American Indian Epic." In *James Fenimore Cooper: New Critical Essays*. Edited by Robert Clark. New York: Barnes & Noble, 1984.

Martin, Terence. "From the Ruins of History: *The Last of the Mohicans*." *Novel* 2 (Spring 1969): 221–29.

Selected Bibliography

Milder, Robert. "*The Last of the Mohicans* and the New World Fall." *American Literature* 52 (November 1980): 407–29.

Peck, H. Daniel, ed. *New Essays on The Last of the Mohicans*. Cambridge, England: Cambridge University Press, 1992. This volume consists of an introduction by Daniel Peck and the following five essays:

Wayne Franklin, "The Wilderness of Words in *The Last of the Mohicans*"; Terence Martin, "From Atrocity to Requiem: History in *The Last of the Mohicans*"; Nina Baym, "How Men and Women Wrote Indian Stories"; Shirley Samuels, "Generation through Violence: Cooper and the Making of Americans"; and Robert Lawson-Peebles, "The Lesson of the Massacre at Fort William Henry."

Philbrick, Thomas. "*The Last of the Mohicans* and the Sounds of Discord." *American Literature* 43 (March 1971): 25–41.

———. "The Sources of Cooper's Knowledge of Fort William Henry." *American Literature* 36 (May 1964): 209–14.

Ringe, Donald A. "Mode and Meaning in *The Last of the Mohicans*." In *James Fenimore Cooper: New Historical and Literary Contexts*. Edited by W. M. Verhoeven. Amsterdam: The Netherlands: Rodop, 1993, 109–24.

Historical Contexts for *The Last of the Mohicans*

Clark, Robert. *History, Ideology, and Myth in American Fiction*, 1823–1852. New York: St. Martin's Press, 1984.

Ferguson, Robert A. *Law and Letters in American Culture*. Cambridge, Mass.: Harvard University Press, 1984.

Gipson, Lawrence H. *The Great War For Empire*, vol. 7. New York: Alfred A. Knopf, 1949.

Gollin, Gillian L. *Moravians in Two Worlds*. New York: Columbia University Press, 1967.

Graymont, Barbara. *The Iroquois in the American Revolution*. Syracuse, N.Y.: Syracuse University Press, 1972.

Hamilton, Edward P. *The French and Indian Wars*. New York: Doubleday, 1962.

Jennings, Francis. *The Ambiguous Iroquois Empire*. New York: W. W. Norton, 1984.

Kolodny, Annette. "Among the Indians: The Uses of Captivity." *New York Times Book Review*. 31 January 1993, 1, 26–29.

Leach, Douglas E. *Arms for Empire*. New York: Macmillan, 1973.

Lukacs, Georg. *The Historical Novel* (1937). Introduction by Frederic Jameson. Lincoln: University of Nebraska Press, 1983.

Maddox, Lucy. *Removals: Nineteenth Century American Literature and the Politics of Indian Affairs*. New York and Oxford: Oxford University Press, 1991.

Meyers, Marvin. *The Jacksonian Persuasion*. Stanford, Calif.: Stanford University Press, 1960.

Pargellis, Stanley. *Lord Loudon in North America*. New Haven, Conn.: Yale University Press, 1933.

Parkman, Francis. *Montcalm and Wolfe* in *France and England in North America*, vol. 2. Notes and Chronology by David Levin. New York: Library of America, 1983.

Prucha, Francis Paul. *American Indian Policy in the Formative Years*. Cambridge, Mass.: Harvard University Press, 1962.

Rogin, Michael. *Fathers and Children: Andrew Jackson and the Subjugation of the American Indian*. New York: Alfred A. Knopf, 1975.

Steele, Ian K. *Betrayals: Fort William Henry and the "Massacre."* Oxford: Oxford University Press, 1990.

Van Der Beets, Richard. *Held Captive by Indians: Selected Narratives, 1642–1836*. Knoxville: University of Tennessee Press, 1973.

White, Richard. *The Middle Ground: Indians, Empires, and Republics in the Great Lakes Region 1650–1815*. Cambridge and New York: Cambridge University Press, 1991.

Index

Index

The Author

John McWilliams is Abernethy Professor of American Literature at Middlebury College in Middlebury, Vermont. His books include *Political Justice in a Republic: James Fenimore Cooper's America* (1972), *Hawthorne, Melville, and the National Character: "A Looking-Glass Business"* (1984), and *The Epic in America: Transforming a Genre, 1770–1860* (1989). With George Dekker, he has coedited *Fenimore Cooper: The Critical Heritage* (1973), and he has edited the Oxford University Press edition of *The Last of the Mohicans* (1994). McWilliams has received a Humanities Institute Fellowship and fellowships from the National Endowment for the Humanities. He has taught at the University of California at Berkeley, the University of Illinois at Chicago, and the University of Maryland. He is at present working on a book about New England historiography.